RVEY L

Setting Up and Facilitating Bereavement Support Groups

WITHDRAWN

by the same author

Talking With Bereaved People
An Approach for Structured and Sensitive Communication
Dodie Graves
ISBN 978 1 84310 988 4
eISBN 978 0 85700 162 7

of related interest

The Essential Guide to Life After Bereavement
Beyond Tomorrow
Judy Carole Kauffmann and Mary Jordan
Foreword by Ciaran Devane
ISBN 978 1 84905 335 8
eISBN 978 0 85700 669 1

After the Suicide
Helping the Bereaved to Find a Path from Grief to Recovery
Kari Dyregrov, Einar Plyhn and Gudrun Dieserud
Foreword by John R. Jordan
ISBN 978 1 84905 211 5
eISBN 978 0 85700 445 1

Writing in Bereavement
A Creative Handbook
Jane Moss
ISBN 978 1 84905 212 2
eISBN 978 0 85700 450 5
Writing for Therapy or Personal Development series

Effective Grief and Bereavement Support
The Role of Family, Friends, Colleagues, Schools and Support Professionals
Kari Dyregrov and Atle Dyregrov
Foreword by Magne Raundalen
ISBN 978 1 84310 667 8
eISBN 978 1 84642 833 3

Silent Grief
Living in the Wake of Suicide. Revised Edition
Christopher Lukas and Henry M. Seiden
ISBN 978 1 84310 847 4
eISBN 978 1 84642 610 0

Talking with Children and Young People about Death and Dying
2nd edition
Mary Turner
Illustrated by Bob Thomas
ISBN 978 1 84310 441 4
eISBN 978 1 84642 560 8

Setting Up and Facilitating Bereavement Support Groups

A Practical Guide

Dodie Graves

Jessica Kingsley *Publishers*
London and Philadelphia

First published in 2012
by Jessica Kingsley Publishers
116 Pentonville Road
London N1 9JB, UK
and
400 Market Street, Suite 400
Philadelphia, PA 19106, USA

www.jkp.com

Copyright © Dodie Graves 2012
Printed digitally since 2013

Library of Congress Cataloging in Publication Data
Graves, Dodie.
  Setting up and facilitating bereavement support groups : a practical guide / Dodie
Graves.
     p. cm.
  Includes bibliographical references and index.
  ISBN 978-1-84905-271-9 (alk. paper)
  1. Bereavement--Psychological aspects. 2. Self-help groups. I. Title.
  BF575.G7G6888 2012
  155.9'37--dc23

                                    2012007765

British Library Cataloguing in Publication Data
A CIP catalogue record for this book is available from the British Library

ISBN 978 1 84905 271 9
eISBN 978 0 85700 573 1

To June, Dave, Liz, Geraldine and Helen for your constancy throughout the years, your commitment to all the participants we meet in our support groups and for providing ideas and advice along the way. Thank you.

Contents

Acknowledgements

I wish to acknowledge those colleagues who have been truly helpful in sharing with me their thoughts, ideas and, in some instances, their practices, for the production of this book. It is fitting that as this is a book written about groups, there should be a group of people involved in the preparation of the material. So to this group of people, I wish to express my grateful thanks. In particular I would like to mention the following: Barbara Burden, for her ongoing support and encouragement; Srinder Singh, at Katherine House Hospice in Banbury, for asking those questions that initiated the discussion on support groups; Jane Pope, at Thorpe Hall Hospice in Peterborough, for providing the Wayfinders leaflet and information about the walking group she started and for much more; Angie Thomas, Nicky, Val, Celia and Sheila, at Cruse Bereavement Care in Birmingham, for sharing with me how they run their many groups; Catherine Betley, from Cruse Head Office, for providing information on the Community Grief Support Programme; Jane Rowley, at Compton Hospice in Wolverhampton, for allowing me to adapt the information they use and for ongoing support; John Orchard, at John Taylor Hospice in Erdington, for guiding my thinking about online groups and answering my many basic questions; Tracy Brailsford and Sue Crittenden, at Ashgate Hospice in Chesterfield, for sharing their experiences; Lesley Whittaker, from Stoke-on-Trent, for sharing some words about pastoral ministry teams in churches; my colleagues in the Midlands and Trent region of the Association of Bereavement Service Co-ordinators (ABSCo), for their enthusiasm and support for this work; Val O'Garro, for excellent supervision; and not least, Lindy and Karen, who gave me their stories of their online encounters. Finally, my thanks again goes to my husband, Charles, for carefully reading the manuscript and for the way he endured the intrusion of all these groups into our home, and without whose support and patience I could not have completed the task.

Disclaimer

All the illustrations used in the book, unless otherwise stated, are composite pictures and any resemblance to people living or dead is coincidental. The dialogue in the case studies is fictional, though the approaches used are based on the practice of a number of groups running in different organizations.

Introduction

Professionals who work in the area of bereavement often talk about group work and how 'to do it'. This almost presupposes that there is a way of doing it that is right. However, the more I have talked to colleagues and worked with groups myself, the more I believe that groups are as varied as the type of people who facilitate them, the settings in which they operate and the people who attend them. Because those who are facilitating groups come from various backgrounds, such as social workers, counsellors and pastoral support workers in places of worship, to name a few, there will be various emphases and different ideas about how to manage groups for people who are bereaved.

Some of the settings in which groups for bereaved people are run include hospices, bereavement support agencies like Cruse and other independent agencies in the voluntary sector, funeral directors, and places of worship. The most recent setting where I have run groups has been a hospice with limited space for such meetings. When I first led groups we had to book multi-purpose rooms that were not altogether suitable, until a refurbishment happily meant we had to move out of the main site to a satellite a quarter of a mile away. It was here we were allocated some rooms that included a sizeable room for group sessions. At the main site it had been most stressful trying to obtain space on a regular basis so as to offer consecutive weeks in the same room. Familiarity with the surroundings, I have realized, can be important for people who may be disoriented by their grief.

Groups may be run structurally in different ways:

- *Closed groups* run with a certain number of people and, once they have started, they are closed to further membership.

- *Open groups* allow for people to join at any time and for others to leave when they feel the time is right to do so or when they choose to opt out.

- *Time-limited groups* run for a certain amount of time, for example weekly for eight sessions or fortnightly for twelve sessions.

- *Ongoing groups* run without an end time in view.

- There are *social groups, self-help groups, drop-in groups*, groups that meet for *creative work* or for more formalized therapeutic *grief work*, and groups that meet with or without an *agenda*.

As indicated above, it may well depend on the experience of the facilitators and their own professional backgrounds as to how they choose to run a group. A variety of groups are available with many skilled people running them very successfully. In this book I discuss how some of these groups operate and how to set them up. It is not my intention to recommend or suggest that one type of group is better than another, though I hope to be able to offer some practical pointers in considering the advantages and disadvantages of each one.

What I have attempted to do in the body of the book is to open up the 'workings' of groups so that those who might not have tried to set up groups before might think about how it can be done and perhaps get some experience in doing it. It might also assist those who already work with groups to consider their practice and perhaps try new methods. So I have attempted to promote some thinking in this area and to raise questions, rather than provide all the answers. This certainly is not a definitive work on the subject of bereavement support groups, but I hope it will provoke further discussion and dialogue. I have also not attempted to include group work with children as there is much already written on that subject and my experience of running groups with children is quite limited.

I will now provide a brief summary of what is contained in each chapter. In Chapter 1, I outline some thinking and planning that I suggest can be profitably done ahead of starting a group, so that you can avoid some potential mishaps. Though be assured, even the most experienced of practitioners still get caught out with new situations and different factors that often require thinking on the hoof. Preparation goes a long way in helping to make a successful group experience both for those who attend and for those who facilitate a group. So in Chapter 1, I look at the initial decision to run a group and some of the considerations to take into account before you even have the first contact.

When we think of leading or facilitating groups, we would be well advised to spend time considering how to *do* certain things and how to *be* in these roles. In Chapter 2, I explore the important question of who runs the group and what type of skills they need to do this. The focus is on what is required of a facilitator and what type of functions the facilitator might wish to perform. In Chapter 3, I provide fictional case studies of two types of groups, a closed group and an open group. Though fictional in description and detail, they are based on a number of groups that have been running over many years with the assistance of some specially trained support workers. I am particularly familiar with the type of time-limited, closed group that has been run at the hospice where I am based. However, as stated before, it is my intention to present ways that different groups operate, and I have done this with the help of some of the professionals who have the experience and expertise in running them. There is also a discussion on special focus groups, creative groups and, with the advancement of technology, the use of online facilities.

In Chapter 4, I discuss the dynamics that you might find in any group, where there are challenges for us as we try to manage the time and 'air-space' for all participants and their needs in a group setting. There can be some challenging behaviours that may potentially threaten the life of the group. People often leave a group where there is weak leadership or where it is not safe to be vulnerable, or where they simply do not have a chance to speak and to connect with others.

In Chapter 5, I examine some pitfalls you might encounter when trying to meet people's needs and especially when supporting people who are hurting. I have found in over 20 years of working with groups that there will always be surprises and you can never be complacent about facilitating a group. Invariably you will encounter things you have not tackled before and these may be the times of best learning for you.

A brief word now regarding the terminology in the book: I have used the word 'participant' to describe the person who joins a group; this is in part a shorthand way of describing the 'group member'. The term 'participant' can also help us think in formal ways about the group members so that we do not overstep some of the boundaries with them. The group members are people who need to 'participate' in order to gain something out of the process. They are not there to be 'recipients' of something that is done for them. It would be your aim to provide a safe place in which participants can think about adjusting to the new order of their world, and to consider some ways of adapting to their 'new normal' lifestyle.

The term I use for the group leader is 'facilitator', which helps to think about the function of the leader, who is in a kind of partnership with the participants, assisting them to share together but keeping the group organized. The facilitator is offering the participants an opportunity to share and to gain support from one another; they are not necessarily teaching, directing or controlling, though at times it might be that some of these aspects emerge through the process. Although I use the word 'run' in relation to a group, I am not making a case here for leadership that is directive or formally structured; I am using this as shorthand for making a group available and for facilitating the process.

If you have never run a group before, this book will provide you with points to consider and ways of going about it. You may have been asked to take over a group that has already been running for some time, and I hope you will find some support for the venture as you read about some of the things that can happen to long-running groups. If you have been facilitating groups for some time, it is my hope that you may find in these pages some ideas you can adapt.

Running groups can be intimidating and can even undermine our confidence if we have been in a group that was not successful. Can someone be helped in knowing how to run groups? Are there ways of working with groups that can be profitably shared with those who are starting out as well as those who have been running groups for years?

I hope this book will go some way to answering those questions, and providing a practical look at what running groups is about, so as to remove some of the mystique surrounding it. I think that it will also raise more questions for you as you think through the issues I have presented. However, knowing the questions can be helpful – it can be halfway to finding the answers.

This book will disappoint those who are looking for a theoretical framework and lots of references. It is not that I have ignored this aspect of study; it is simply that the people I have talked to who would use a book such as this have wanted the practicalities of setting up and facilitating groups and not the theory. I hope it will not disappoint them. I have turned to some professionals for advice on managing difficult behaviours as I wanted to compare and augment what I do in practice with what is suggested by those who are more practised and have expertise in this area.

It is my hope that if you are running bereavement support groups you might feel free to experiment with different types of groups that will match your own strengths with the needs of those who have been bereaved, and not feel the need to 'get it right'.

CHAPTER 1

Setting Up a Bereavement Support Group

There seems to be some mystique around the practice of running groups for bereaved people, a feeling that there is somehow a right way and a wrong way of doing it. I was in conversation with someone from another bereavement agency who said she did not think she could run groups because they were fairly intimidating. I agreed with her; they can, in fact, be quite scary. Every time I work with a new group I experience a level of anxiety and not a little nervousness as I sit in front of six to eight people, all waiting for me to start. This is in part because I know they are people who are hurting and are all, at some point, likely to well up in tears or react in quite unexpected ways. The expectation of me is much greater somehow than when I am sitting in front of one person who is relating their story to me, allowing me time to think about this person and this person alone. In a group you have many more people to think about and more stories to assimilate; you have names to remember and the names of all the deceased and their circumstances; and you have different personalities to handle.

Facilitating a group, then, can be quite daunting. In another setting, a very competent and skilful counsellor told me he would not run groups because, when he had tried, the group had disintegrated and fallen apart. He felt he did not have the skills and the confidence to handle a group, and yet on a one-to-one level he was excellent.

It is important to say at the outset that there is no shame in not running groups if it is not for you. Just as groups are not for everybody to join and participate in, so groups are not for every counsellor or skilled social worker or pastoral worker to run. Facilitating groups requires different skills from supporting individuals on a one-to-one basis. Groups require people who are skilled enough to handle all the various things that happen in a group. It is my opinion that there should always be a trained and skilled person who is responsible for the group at the level of supervision and support, especially in a situation where the running of the group has been delegated to volunteers or other professionals.

SOME THINGS TO CONSIDER BEFORE YOU START

Before you start planning to run a group, there are some major considerations to take on board. Good preparation ahead of time will help the practical arrangements go smoothly and the participants will be more confident in the process. As I have already stated, groups are not for everyone, which is what I say to prospective participants before a group starts. Attending a group can be daunting for some people to contemplate, while for others it becomes a lifeline. Some people will ask you what a group is about, or what goes on in a group; some will want to know what the advantages are for themselves, or what benefits they will gain from attending. Some will be grateful for the company but not be aware of the expectation on them to share at an emotional level; some will not be able to attend all the group sessions (for a closed group) and so change the dynamics due to their intermittent attendance. There are, then, some major considerations to take into account. There are also advantages and disadvantages for the organization to consider.

With these few thoughts in mind, I will examine in more detail some of the things you will need to reflect on. I start with some of the advantages and disadvantages that might exist for the organization and then I look at what might be advantageous or otherwise for the participants.

Advantages for your organization

- You may be able to support more people in groups than on a one-to-one basis. This means it is more cost-effective for the organization, such as having two facilitators for a larger number of participants. In this age of cost consciousness it may be a selling point for your organization in terms of numbers seen and people helped.

- If the organization is able to run groups with skilled volunteers, it is also more cost-effective than tying up the professionals' time. This frees the professionals to do other tasks and fulfil other roles.

- The organization does not have to provide someone experienced in every type of grief; the participants will seek answers from one another. The participants often support each other without looking to the facilitator for the answers; they are grateful for the opportunity to share with others who are in a similar situation to themselves.

- The organization can gain a higher profile in the local community by providing groups, as people will start to be informed about the opportunities available for this activity.

Disadvantages for your organization

- A significant disadvantage to the organization is the time commitment needed by at least two staff or volunteers over a period of time. It is hard to miss a session as it affects the continuity of the group working and may affect the way the members relate to you.

- It can be difficult to find an appropriate room big enough on a weekly or fortnightly basis for a length of time.

- Other staff in the organization need to be aware of the group and buy into the importance of not interrupting, not wandering in by mistake or intentionally, or not making a noise in the corridors.

- You can still be required to provide individual work either before or after a group, which can be time consuming. Participants may have received support before attending the group, and then afterwards (if it is a closed group) they may request support on a one-to-one basis. This will require further assessment and provision of support if necessary.

- Some participants can find the experience too overwhelming for them and will not return after the first session. If it is a closed group, this can affect the group's functioning, so it is good to have a waiting list if possible. The facilitators have to work hard at getting a group started in these circumstances. It may not have a major impact on those in an open group as participants come and go more frequently.

These are just a few of the major advantages and disadvantages to the organization when you are thinking about running a group.

Advantages for the participants

When you are talking to prospective participants, it is helpful to explain some of the advantages and disadvantages so that they can think about what is involved in joining a group and be prepared. Here are some of the advantages you might offer them:

- Coming together can mean they can socialize and support each other outside the group meetings. The participants might find they make some new social contacts and widen their support network. (Although some organizations do not offer social events for the bereaved group, participants may take it upon themselves to call each other and make their own arrangements. This can evolve over time.)

- The participant can hear other people's opinions and points of view that may be similar to or different from their own, and hence they are able to assess their own situations in the light of others' experiences. They may well benefit from a discussion on a certain matter or take advice from each other.

- They may also be able to reassure themselves that they are not going mad. This is a common fear for bereaved people as they can experience very different emotions and ideas from their normal ways of being, feeling and thinking and can find themselves behaving in what they think are strange ways. 'I think I'm losing it' is often said with the hope of getting the reassurance that they are not abnormal and that what they are experiencing is fairly usual, given their circumstance. It is reassuring to hear other people in similar situations voicing the same fears and talking about the same reactions.

- They have a set time that takes them out of the house and away from their situations which may be of benefit in bringing some perspective to their own circumstances.

- They might be able to raise issues not raised with family or friends because they are in a safe environment where other people understand and will not be offended.

Disadvantages for the participants

Realistically, there are some negatives for the participants too, which need to be explained before they decide to come to a group. Here are some of the important disadvantages to consider:

- They will not have the same amount of 'air-space' or time to speak as they would if they had an hour's visit with a bereavement support worker. They will have to share the time with others.

- They will hear other people's stories and they may feel burdened by these as well as their own story when they leave the group, especially after the first few sessions. This is quite a consideration for them as they have enough sadness and distress in their own lives to handle without taking on the worries and concerns of others. Most people, it has to be said, find they are able to bear with others' sorrows and are able to be compassionate towards one another without sinking under the weight of them. There are those who are not able to do so, however, and they quickly make this plain, so it is important to be clear and offer them the alternative of individual support, if at all possible.

- They may not like the other people in the group, or there might be a participant who starts to dominate the group discussions. Explain to them that this will be dealt with by the group facilitators but that they have to go through the experience before it can be handled and it may be handled outside the group rather than inside.

- It may be daunting, especially the first time they come, as they are usually nervous, not knowing what to expect with the prospect of meeting strangers.

- In a closed group, it can be disruptive in the initial sessions if there are comings and goings when people have not arrived as you expected them to, so it takes longer to settle into the work of the group and the life of it. I usually explain to the participants that this can happen so that they might expect a little change in the make-up of the group before they settle down for the rest of the time allocated. (A group itself may make a decision about attendance at the first meeting, and it may be an issue if someone is not totally committed to attending.)

Of course, we do not want to discourage people from attending, but we do need to explain what may happen for them and prepare them ahead of time so that they have a more realistic picture of what they are coming into and signing up for. They can then make an informed decision to attend or not.

An illustration of this is the case of Mark. I spoke to Mark on several occasions over the period of time before a new group was to begin. He began by insisting that he wanted to attend a group, but in fact I was not very certain that he would be able to benefit from the experience. Mark seemed to be an anxious person and there appeared to be something a little diffident about the way he presented himself. This prompted me to offer him the opportunity of a one-off session with a group facilitator who would talk to him about the way the group would operate (covering many of the details I have outlined above). At the same time he could tell his story prior to attending the group, if he still wanted to. During that session with the group facilitator he made his mind up not to come to a group but to have one-to-one support at his own home, where he was in control and comfortable. There are people who are nervous or anxious and probably would find attending a group too overwhelming and would drop out almost immediately. I believe these people might benefit more from seeing a support worker for individual work before they think of attending a group. After they have had some support on an individual basis, they may be in a stronger position to choose whether to attend a group or not; in this way they are able to use the experience more constructively for themselves.

Having thought about the advantages and disadvantages for the organization and the positives and negatives for the participants, we will turn our thinking to the particular type of group to be run. The choice of group may be dictated by the capacity you have in terms of skilled facilitators and the time they have available, the venue and its availability, the location and any other number of other constraints.

Open or closed groups

Whether to have an open or closed group is a decision that you may want to make after reading the case studies in Chapter 3, as there are advantages and disadvantages in running both. Many organizations run closed groups that meet weekly or fortnightly, and many run open groups that meet fortnightly or monthly. It can also be that you run both, perhaps moving people on from a closed, time-limited group to an open group that meets less frequently and is less formal but meets on an ongoing basis.

Aims of a group

It would be advantageous to get your aims clear in your mind as to the kind of group you are able to offer, before you even speak to any prospective participants. The aims you have will influence your style of leading and organization of the group; the facilitation mode – whether or not you are going to do any teaching or give input or any other way of operating; and the facilities and amenities you will require to accommodate such a group appropriately. An example of getting your aims clearly in mind would be about whether or not you target a particular group of people with specific needs, for example a group of young widowed men and women under a certain age, or a group of parents whose adult child has died. Or you may make a decision that every type of bereavement and relationship will be invited to the same group. Another decision would be about how to assess the participants for their suitability. It may be that you decide you will not assess anyone and will accept everyone who arrives for the group on a given day. Whoever is responsible for the overall running of the group and the participants' well-being will need to be part of the decision-making process and on board with the way the group proceeds at every session.

Types of groups

There are some major differences between the types of groups that run which you need to be clear about before you begin. I believe the major differences exist between therapeutic, support and self-help groups. Each organization may have their own interpretation of these, but I will set out my own way of defining them, so that you will know the type of group I am discussing in the following chapters.

Therapeutic groups

A therapeutic group is one that runs for people who have identified that they have specific personal problems that impact their grieving, or their general practitioner (GP) has identified with them an issue that seems to be impeding a normal adjustment and adaptation to grief and loss. These problems might be around specific issues of grief or family dynamics and the individual's way of relating to them. They would be more complex issues than the majority of people experiencing grief might present. For instance, they may have issues related to drug or alcohol dependency or some other pre-existing issue that is complicated further by the bereavement. The way of running this type of group would be to focus on the specific issues and help the participants work out how the issues are impacting them, how they themselves are impacting the issues or impacting other people, and how they might resolve the issues. This type of group has much more the feel of a psychological therapy group, and they would be run by trained professional staff. The aim of this group and the type of group member who is eligible for participation should be clearly thought through. For example, do you take into the group those with diagnosed mental illnesses or personality disorders? How would you be made aware of these issues in order to make your assessment? Do you have facilitators qualified and experienced in these areas to offer space to people with those needs?

Support groups

A support group is usually a group where people come to discuss their bereavement, perhaps the issues around the death, their emotional well-being, and their strategies for coping. People who sign up for this type of group generally want to hear from others in a similar situation, and they are willing to share and hear what others have to say. They are usually run by trained staff and volunteers.

Self-help groups

A self-help group is similar in some respects to a support group, but whereas a support group might be focused on the emotional issues, a self-help group might be focused on the more practical issues of bereavement, sharing ways of coping and helping each other out. A self-help group may also be run by someone who is bereaved themselves and is willing to support others. In practice, the self-help group and the support group may overlap in the content and style of operating, though differ in the leadership.

Social groups

A social group exists solely to provide opportunities for people who are bereaved to get together in order to have social interaction. It may well be, of course, that during those interactions people talk about their grieving process, how they are coping and the difficulties they face. The main intention of the group is to organize social events, particularly to alleviate the loneliness and isolation which many bereaved spouses or partners feel. However, because they may be sharing at deep levels, you may wish to consider who should be involved in hosting this type of group, and what type of training in listening skills and bereavement they should have before they get involved.

Other groups

Other groups operate on a 'drop-in' basis where the leaders will need to decide what approach they take for people who are there one week and not there the next, and maybe they have not had any previous contact with the participants, so little is known beforehand. A drop-in group could be a support group, a self-help group or a social group, but would need defining so that participants know what to expect.

Other groups meet for creative work over a period of time or as a one-off day or session. The creative activities might include making a piece of work that fits into a whole, like making ceramic tiles that are then put together to make up a whole picture, or there might be a number of various creative activities that are independent of each other. There are groups that meet together for more formalized 'grief work' done through creative exercises or activities that aid the client in talking through their issues.

Regardless of whether the group is closed or open, groups can meet either with a programme offering different topics, or structured content to discuss each week, or meet without a fixed agenda.

A cautionary tale

Whatever type of group you are going to run, it needs to be described and defined for the sake of both the facilitators and the participants, who will need to decide if they can sign up to such an activity. Here is an illustration of how *not* to do it and what the consequences were:

> My first attempt to run a creative day went horribly wrong; it seemed that I had not fully explained that the activities would require the participants to think about their grief and to depict this in a creative way, using collage or paints. So on the day, there were four people who refused to do a particular exercise because one of them had begun to find it too distressful. The other three became protective of her and downed tools in sympathy. I had to save the day by talking them through their complaints (in a side room away from the clients who were working on the given exercise) and was able to negotiate with them that they could do something a little more 'fun'. Thinking fast on my feet and drawing from my school art classes, I set up a still-life for them, which gave them pleasure and fun as they were able to laugh at their attempts.

I learnt from that experience that people would not automatically understand what they are being invited to take part in, so my next attempt was much more structured and better described in the advertising flyer.

Getting people in

To make a group function you have to have a minimum number of participants and this can sometimes prove problematic. You have to have a fairly large number of people to draw from in the first instance. Hospices and places of worship are able to send out letters or brochures after a death, advertising the group meetings, because they have access to the bereaved relatives. Some places of worship will have details of bereaved relatives as a result of a funeral that has been conducted by the leader. These details may be passed on to a pastoral team who may visit the main mourner's family, at which time group leaflets are left with them, or leaflets are sent to them through the mail. Other agencies rely on self-referrals from advertising in public places, or from doctors' referrals. In those situations the person might be assessed and the possibility of a group offered if it is felt it would be suitable for them. Some organizations will offer individual support first with an option to join a group at a later stage.

As far as advertising is concerned, it may be possible to link up with a number of local funeral directors so that they offer your group leaflets or flyers to the families they see. If you wish to run an open group, this can be a good way of recruiting. It may be best to design your information so that they need to contact you before arriving at the group venue (unless you are providing a drop-in service). This will help with assessing the suitability of the person and give you some idea of their situation, the type of death as well as some details of the deceased and the bereaved person. It may also help in planning the sessions ahead if you are aware that new people are likely to come and the numbers you will need to cater for.

So, in order to recruit, you may have to send out information ahead of time, unless you are recruiting from clients who are being seen on an individual basis and you are able to offer an invitation to them to join a group. One organization that offers closed groups sends out a leaflet that gives information about the type of group they run and what the bereaved person can expect. The leaflet provides information about who will lead the group, the times and dates of the next group and a tear-off slip to be returned, with provision for the bereaved person's telephone number so they can be contacted if they are interested in attending (see Appendix 1). You may also have to think about where you advertise your group, because if you put up posters in all the doctors' surgeries, libraries and supermarkets in your area, you might be inundated with requests that will take a lot of handling. If you wish to run closed groups, you will be required to work out how to select the number you can run with, and what criteria to use to do so.

If you are running open groups, you may have to have premises that cater for a larger-size group. A practical option for working with larger numbers is to have a short address on a topic and then to break the larger group down into smaller subgroups of similar death types, for example those bereaved of a spouse or partner, those bereaved of a young child, those bereaved of an adult child, those bereaved of a parent, and so on. It also may be that those bereaved by suicide or murder would be better served by being referred to special focus groups that run with specially trained group facilitators in those areas (further discussion of this is in Chapter 3).

In some organizations closed groups are offered over a period of two to three months, and so it is theoretically possible to run groups three or four times a year, or more if daytime and evening groups are running concurrently. Some organizations run with two ongoing, open groups where one meets in the daytime and one meets in the evening. Those who opt to run closed groups will need to accept that there will be times when there are so few participants signed up that the group cannot run. It may be necessary to set dates ahead for the groups so that the facilitators are booked in and can avoid taking their holidays in those weeks, and that rooms are booked in advance. Alternatively, you may wish to wait until you have a feasible number of people to run a group and then arrange the times and dates. This will depend on your own systems and flexibility with regard to resources and facilitators. If you set up a time-limited, closed group there may be one or two participants in a group who have a date they cannot manage because of another commitment, but if they can manage to make at least the majority of the sessions, you may wish to offer them a place. If they cannot make a good number of sessions, it might be advisable to discuss with them whether it is more beneficial for them to consider attending the next group that will run.

Suitability

If you are running open groups or drop-in groups, you may choose not to have selection criteria, or do assessments. If you are running closed groups, likewise you may choose to do assessments or not. Personally, I believe there are people who are not right for a group for many reasons. I remember in my counselling training doing a module on group work, and the professor actually shocked me by saying, 'Remember, the group is more important than the individual.' I was taken aback I suppose because of wanting to care for the individuals who are in a position of need. However, over the years, I have come to value that piece of advice. If there are people in the group who will harm the life of the group, they need to be deselected and offered other alternatives. Here is an illustration of how I dealt with a situation where the participant was unsuitable.

> Barbara came to one of our groups for one time only. She had proved to be difficult to talk to over the phone as she did not appear to be listening to what I was saying and was intent on telling me about her involvement with the community, the council and other action groups. I especially wanted her to hear the point about being in a group and giving everyone space to talk and not having one person dominate. She clearly thought she knew what that meant, even saying she knew she talked a lot but would respect others' points of view. I was not totally convinced, however.
>
> At the debriefing after the first session, the two facilitators were absolutely exhausted and tucking into the chocolate biscuits – I knew something had gone wrong! Barbara had not even allowed them to complete the ground rules before jumping in and taking over. The facilitators had done a valiant job in attempting to contain her but they were concerned that she would deter the other participants from attending. She kept on insisting that she was different, and in fact the facilitators did think she was in a different place from the other participants, as she was very keen to be involved in action groups and committees rather than share her feelings with the group.
>
> With some trepidation I called Barbara that afternoon. We had discussed that I should explain that we thought the group was

probably not right for her as she was in a different place with her grief compared with the others and she might benefit from having individual support from me. Barbara was well aware that she was different and accepted the offer of support on an ad hoc basis, as she told me she was very busy.

We needed to help Barbara see that this group was not suitable for her, without causing her too much distress. The point is that the group is more important than the individual, otherwise the group may fail if the individual proves too difficult for the group to manage. The answer to this one might have been for me *not* to have accepted her for the group in the first place, and with hindsight I should have done a home visit and made a greater attempt to demonstrate to her how a group would probably not be beneficial for her. It is really difficult to see how people will be together in a group too, so I think there will always be these trial and error situations.

Selection criteria

Before you start you may wish to have selection criteria in place. These may be based on age, gender, the type of relationship and the time since the death, all of which can be justified if you are running certain types of groups. Sometimes deafness and profound deafness can be a concern unless the person who is deaf is adept at managing group situations. If someone is deaf, I ask them what environments are more difficult for them to cope with, and it will usually be in groups of people. I then talk through what happens in a group, and how important it is to be able to hear what is going on for the other participants, as people who are distressed often talk in low voices. The person can be helped to feel that this is not discriminatory but is actually for their own comfort and the comfort of the other participants. Individual support may be a better and more satisfactory option for them.

Another consideration would be the time elapsed from the death. Some organizations offer group work only to those who have been bereaved for longer than five to six months. The reason given for this is that, in their experience, those in the early months after a death find it more difficult to process their grief in a constructive way in a group. For some people the experience can be too daunting, especially in telling the story of the events leading up to the death of their loved one. So part of your thinking prior to setting up a group could be whether you want to set any time frames. The advantage for people who are all bereaved for more than a period of six months is that they are likely to be experiencing similar things together, whereas in early grief there is a vulnerability that can be too painful to share.

Assessments

Having selection criteria in place might be helpful and, in the same way, doing assessments before placing people in a group might be beneficial to both parties. As I have stated previously, if you have advertised your groups in public places and run open or drop-in groups for the community, you may choose not to do assessments. However, if you are thinking about assessments, they can be done over the telephone and so do not have to be too time consuming. They can, of course, also be done on a face-to-face basis, either at the person's home or at the organization. In any case, your understanding of the prospective participant's situation and how they are coping can be helped by going over several areas of their story and circumstances. In addition it is wise to listen carefully to how they are presenting their stories to you. I use an assessment process that enables me to get into their stories through a number of prepared questions. Here are some examples of the type of questions you can ask, and the rationale behind them.

- What is your family situation? Who is there in the family now that you can turn to? Who would you say your closest friends are now? How are they supporting you at this time? (In both these areas you are looking for people in the support network who might be available to give assistance, and you are looking at the level of isolation.)

- What would you think is your biggest struggle now? How do you think you're coping with your loss? What emotions are you experiencing? (These questions give them the opportunity to share their emotional struggle and to try to put into words what it is they are finding hard to come to terms with.)

- Some people find they're using alcohol or food to try to cope with the stress: have you found you're doing things like drinking more than you used to? Or eating more or less than before (or smoking more, if they are a smoker)? (This is a way of getting some of the more difficult questions out into the open, something that they might not have wanted to disclose but feel encouraged to do so by a direct question.)

- I wonder if you would feel able to explain briefly to me the circumstances of your husband's (wife's, etc.) illness (or death). (Although this is a closed statement or question, most people are willing to talk about their experience, unless they feel too emotional to do so. I ask it in this way, because I am not able to ascertain where they are emotionally if I make the contact by telephone. Also, if they have people with them, they may not wish to talk about this. However, it is helpful to hear the story of the illness and death so that you can ascertain how they have viewed it, whether it was a shock, or an expected death. In circumstances where a death was not expected, it is as well to know what you are dealing with so that you can help the client think through whether a mixed group is suitable for them or whether a specific focus group would be more beneficial.)

- Have you had any support or counselling before in any other circumstances in your life? (It is helpful to be aware of someone's history in this area, as it may reveal that they have experienced mental health issues and this can be discussed, if you have raised the topic.)

- Have you ever been part of a support group before for anything? Are you attending another support group for your bereavement at the moment? If they have: What was the experience like for you and what did you value from it? If they are currently in a group, you might wish to explore this further and find out what they think the benefit of attending your group might be, and any overlaps and issues of confidentiality they could see arising. (Further discussion on this is given below.)

- Are there any difficulties you might have in hearing or sight that we might need to take into consideration? (If you have a venue with stairs but no lift you may have to ask about their ability to manage stairs.)

Assessments are only a limited aid in checking out the suitability of the prospective participant as it can be difficult to assess how the individuals you have seen will all get along when put together in a group. Having some criteria in place may help, though, when having to make some awkward decisions, before you find yourself face to face with something you were not prepared for.

Attending more than one group

As raised above, an issue to consider is whether you are comfortable with people going to different bereavement groups in the same town at the same time as attending one of your groups. Borne out of some experience, I now make sure the participant understands that they do not use the one group to complain about the other group; nor should they bring in any confidential information from that other group, or make comparisons between the groups in or outside the sessions with us. If you wish to make a policy that they should attend only one group at a time, be aware this might cause offence as it could be seen as an infringement of their rights to choose what they do with their own time. On one occasion, after I thought I had carefully pointed out a possible concern about attending two groups to a prospective participant, I was told in no uncertain terms that I could not stop her going to both groups. Her contention was that if she wanted and needed this sort of contact on a regular basis, and if it was helping her, I had no right to prevent her getting that support. It was carefully put, but I got the message loud and clear, and in actual fact this woman kept the groups quite separate during her attendance at our closed group. However, you might wish to retain the 'right' to decide whether or not you, or the organization, will work with someone who is already attending a group.

Homogeneous or mixed types of death or relationship

A question that often arises around group work is whether groups should have a specific membership (e.g. younger people bereaved of a spouse or partner, or older bereaved widows and widowers or partners) or whether groups of people bereaved of a young child or an adult child or a parent or a sibling or any other relationship can meet together. Some organizations have experienced a withdrawal of participants who have not shared the same relationship as the majority of the group (e.g. a predominance of widows, widowers or partners with a participant whose parent has died). This can be for several reasons: the issues discussed around the loss of a partner or a spouse might not feel relevant to the participant whose relationship is different. Talking about a change of role or the way friends react to their loss and the ensuing social isolation, or their feelings of rejection, might not be helpful to a mother whose adult child has died, or a daughter whose father has died. Another reason for the drop-out might be that they feel guilty at the sessions because they then go home to a spouse or partner and they do not have to face the particular loss the other participants are experiencing.

There are a number of ways to operate with this issue (though in practice I believe it always comes down to the people you have in the group and how they interact). One way would be to hold groups for different relationships at different times, but this presupposes you can get enough of those people together at one time. Another way of handling it would be to have a large number of people who have different losses and to hold plenary sessions followed by smaller subdivided group work so that people whose loss is similar can be together for more specific sharing. You would need to be aware of who is attending so that you do not face having just one person left out on their own. Another suggestion is having the mixed group with different relationships (e.g. spouses and adult children) for the whole session but ensuring that there are more than one of the type of bereavement, otherwise they may not feel they can identify with any one.

Mixed groups are certainly possible to run, but it has proved necessary to ensure that the facilitators point out the similarities and the differences for people who are grieving, regardless of the relationship, at the beginning of the group sessions. After all, even in a homogeneous group, there will always be differences in many factors. These might include the time elapsed from the death; the place of death, whether at home, in a hospice or hospital or in the street or some other public place; the type of death that was experienced and whether expected or not; the causes of death, whether it was a long or short illness or a sudden tragic or violent death; the degree of support that was experienced during the illness and afterwards or at the time of the death by other agencies such as police or paramedics; the age of the deceased; and the type of family involved in the bereavement. So there can already be many differences among participants even if they have all experienced the death of a particular loved one, spouse, partner, child and so on.

I have known of one mixed group made up predominantly of those bereaved of a spouse or partner which was also attended by a woman whose mother had died. This could have been a difficult mix, but the woman talked honestly about her differences, and the rest of the group apparently could see how deeply significant the loss of her mother was and they were willing to support her in this loss. The feedback was that some good learning had occurred for all of those in the group and it was a beneficial time for all the participants. A sense of perspective may be gained, where they experience others who have different stories and different losses, and are moved by the loss for that individual. This is perhaps a reflection of the way loss impacts us in families and there may be a case for having a mix.

In the end it may come down to the resources you have in your organization to handle mixed groups or homogeneous groups, resources such as the number of facilitators and their ability to handle different situations. As to age, it may be difficult to find enough young widows, widowers or partners who want a group at the same time, so you may need to mix the ages. Most of the time it works, as their issue is still the grief, though young people and older people do have different needs.

Evaluation of outcomes

In the current economic climate of trying to obtain funding for community activities, you may wish, or indeed need, to present some evidence-based statistics around the efficacy and benefits of the work with bereaved people in groups. Having a measuring tool that can give some quantifiable evidence of how your participants have benefited from attending will be a necessity. Appendix 2 offers an evaluation form that I have used quite successfully in the past to obtain group feedback, which you may wish to adapt to suit your own needs, though at present it is not quantifiable and is still a work in progress. Because we did not measure where the participants felt they were at the beginning of the group, we have not asked for feedback about where they feel they are at the end of the group sessions. This is something that will be addressed in the future as we experience the different pressures to measure these outcomes.

SOME THINGS TO CONSIDER ABOUT RUNNING THE GROUP

Group size

There is considerable discussion around the question of group size within those agencies that run groups. I have a personal preference for smaller numbers which may be more manageable, allowing more time for each person to speak at some length, where they feel they have had an opportunity to voice their feelings, thoughts and stories without feeling too rushed. The number of participants for that to happen is probably around six to eight and no more than ten, in my experience. Again, it depends on what the aim of the group is and what the expectations of the participants are. Some agencies run with considerably more than that in each group. (This is discussed more fully in Chapter 2.)

Number of sessions

The number of sessions that closed groups run for varies considerably across organizations. Some organizations run groups fortnightly over a period of twelve weeks, which seems to work well. Meeting twice a month gives time for the participants and the facilitators to do other things in their week off, but it also means that the flow of discussion is not too lost. Other organizations run groups for six, eight or ten sessions over consecutive weeks. By running weekly there is an advantage for the flow of the group where issues brought up the previous week can be quickly recalled (or put aside if the group chooses to). Another advantage to running weekly is that the facilitators are not on duty for a longer period of six months or a year. It seems that participants will adapt to what is on offer, but their needs or wants have to be balanced with the available resources you have at your disposal.

As an organization we find eight sessions are workable, though the participants nearly always report that they want more. I would rather they feel they want to continue than the group become stagnated and the participants too dependent on us and the group. If they form a group outside – off our premises – then they can continue for as long as they want. An example of this is a group that has been meeting for four years after they finished their 'official' group, and have gone on holidays together and continue to meet every week.

One organization reports that they had feedback from their closed, time-limited groups requesting a reunion session where groups from the year could come together for a social gathering. This provoked much discussion about the practicalities and the possible advantages or disadvantages of offering such an opportunity. The discussion was around some of these thoughts: as they had not had a social aspect to the groups they offered, this could well be a good time for participants to meet for an informal get-together. However, if several participants of a particular group did not come, the others could have a negative experience. If all the groups were brought together on one occasion, the group facilitators who have led more than one group in a year would be thinly spread around the groups and may not have a meaningful time with any of them. Perhaps too, for some, it may be a retrogressive step to come back to a place or time with so many difficult memories. It was also felt that if the participants wanted to meet outside the organized group, and also after it has finished, they could do so and organize their own reunions.

Timing of a group

There are questions about the timing of groups in relation to the yearly calendar and the school calendar. This is of particular consideration for those running closed, time-limited groups, but not as applicable to the running of open groups. I have found that I need to be mindful of the seasons, especially the Christmas season when there is so much emotional emphasis placed on family life. I have tried various ways around this. One way was to run groups wrapped around the holiday, so that participants can talk about their emotions around Christmas and their plans, and then they can come back after Christmas to catch up on the events and their reactions. One problem I found with this was that the participants would often be away around that time or be very busy and the attendance fell away before the holiday, and then it took time to get going with a full complement afterwards, so the group usually finished rather raggedly. Another way was to finish the group in November so that the season does not come into focus quite so much, other than to discuss how people will cope with it. If you run during half terms and school holidays, this may affect some grandparents who are also heavily involved in looking after their grandchildren and will affect more especially the surviving parent who has to juggle work and holiday activities. Making an evening group available for those who work may be viable, or not, depending on the numbers that respond to make it a feasible group. You may also need to offer different days for each group, and different times in the day, to cater for people's varying commitments.

Having set up the number of weeks, for a closed group, there is then the question of the length of time for each session. Some weekly groups run for an hour and a half plus a little extra for a refreshment break; some run for two hours; some have a morning session followed by lunch. You will need to tailor the length of time you offer according to the aim you have established. If you are running a creative group, for example, where participants are working on a creative project, or are doing several individual creative pieces of work and then discussing them, you may need to offer three to four hours or more. If you are offering a monthly group, you may want to offer a longer session to take into account the fact that people will want more air-space to give an update of what they have been encountering. If you are in a rural area where transport is limited and people have to make an effort to attend from different parts of the county or area, you may wish to have longer sessions, but it might be useful to have the sessions in two parts with refreshments in the middle.

From the point of view of facilitating the group, it can be draining for the facilitators if they are with the participants solidly for two to three hours. If the group is going well, and everyone is contributing and the discussion is flowing, it will be stimulating for them and they will feel positive. If, however, the group is slow to get going or it is a group that brings in their sorrow and pain and the atmosphere hangs heavy, it can be difficult for the facilitators over a few hours. This is one of the reasons for always having two facilitators present in a group. There are other reasons which I will discuss further in Chapter 2.

As already mentioned, there is also the issue of the timing in the grief journey for the participants. A valid question arises about whether you include early bereaved people along with those whose loss is coming up to the first anniversary. Some anecdotal evidence suggests that they do not mix particularly well. The early bereaved people may be affected because they see someone still in grief after a year and they can become despondent about that, as their own expectation might be that they would be in a better place in a year's time. The one who is at an anniversary stage might be reminded again of the depths of pain they experienced as they witness the pain of those in early grief.

As an illustration, I had supported a man for nearly a year after the death of his wife and, though he was making adjustments and was adapting to the new circumstances, he still felt the loneliness and loss and thought a group might offer some extra support for him. He came to the first session and told me afterwards he would not be going back:

> 'I'm not where the others are; they're in such deep grief. Don't get me wrong, I still miss her, but I didn't realize how far I'd come in this year. I think if I come to the group I'll go back down again listening to their stories and their pain.'

This was actually a turning point for him and he was able to stop coming for support.

The decision of whether to mix the group is not an easy one, but depending on the pool of people you are drawing from, you may not get enough people who have been bereaved longer than a year to attend a group as they do not wish to revisit the pain and have decided that they will get on with life as it is. It may well be a different experience for some others, in which case mixing the group may not be a problem; again it may be about the type of people you have in the group, and if it is explained beforehand, they may feel more prepared for the differences.

What should happen in a group?

I was once asked if a group should run itself. This is a question worth some serious consideration. The group 'running itself' suggests that participants are allowed to bring in their own topics for discussion and they take responsibility for the success of the group themselves. However, you might have a number of issues up your sleeve in case there is nothing that seems to be the topic for the day. When I run a group I try to work around the following six elements as a framework: stories of the illness, the death, the funeral and the life of the deceased; the relationship between the deceased and the group participant and the rest of the family; thinking of the ways in which the participant can remember and celebrate the life of the deceased; the emotional and physical legacies the deceased has left behind for the participant and the family; the strategies for coping that the participant is using or not using; and the journey they have been on since the death and where they think their life might be going in the future (Graves 2009). Of course, there are often practical issues that come up that they want to talk through together. Each group has its own agenda and takes a different course from any other group because of it. In this sense the group 'runs itself'.

If, however, 'running itself' means that you simply provide a space and refreshments for them to meet in the organization's facilities without trained facilitators, there may be issues you would want to consider. You might want to consider how you would be able to regulate the group and know it was offering a safe place for vulnerable people. It is possible that people could be more damaged than helped. I am aware of some organizations that allow this to happen after a closed group has run its course and the group then goes on to fulfil a social function, being 'hosted' by trained volunteers, but away from the main premises.

Facilities

In thinking about your aims and what you want to offer your participants, you will need to reflect on the facilities and amenities that you will require or that are available to you. For example, with the best will in the world, you cannot offer a creative group working with paints and other materials if you do not have a sink nearby or tables to sit at. You will also need to think about how many rooms you need, the size of the room (twelve people will not fit comfortably in a room that will seat only eight), whether there is a toilet near by, a place to hang coats, a reception area for early comers to sit in and wait, and a decision about what you do about late comers (having someone available to escort them to the group room). You may need to consider if there are disturbances that might be experienced in your room, and whether the room is soundproofed so that minimum noise is heard from inside by those outside and vice versa. We had a room for a long time that had windows onto the front reception area where ambulances were pulling up. This was quite distressing for some people as it brought back memories of the day they came with their loved one to the hospice.

Refreshments

Here, I would just like to add a thought about refreshments that you might offer, if any. It seems a trivial thing to think about but it could cause some difficulties if not thought through carefully. It can be a sign of hospitality and warmth, inviting people into a place that considers the physical comfort of the participants as well as the emotional. It can also be an ice-breaker for people who are just getting to know each other. People can feel looked after and cared for: as one facilitator reminded me, 'If people are living on their own, it can be a bit of a luxury to have a drink made for them.' If you wish to have drinks, you need to think about the practicalities like a fridge, an urn or a kettle, and staff or volunteers who are responsible for providing refreshments. In some facilities there are areas where participants can meet to have refreshments before the group starts. One organization I know asks participants to leave their coffee cups behind, with cold water and plastic cups being provided in the meeting room. The facilitator I spoke to at this organization felt quite strongly that moving into a different room gives the message that they are now changing gear and doing something deeper than having a chat over coffee. There are certainly different ways of looking at this, and some people would feel more relaxed and more comfortable with a hot drink in their hand. In our previous accommodation in the hospice building, we had kitchen staff who provided our refreshments on a trolley and would bring it in for us. This meant we had to be rigorous in making sure the order went into the kitchen staff for the duration of the group; we were dependent on their memories and their time-keeping.

In this chapter I have shared some of the practical issues I have found worth considering as I have run groups over the years. Most of my understanding about these issues has come from hard lessons, starting off a little naively and blundering into the pitfalls and mistakes which are uncomfortable at the time but help to shape some constructive thinking about supporting bereaved people in groups. In summary, it will be important to start with your aims followed by a realistic examination of the capacity you have to fulfil those aims, which then means you can make decisions about the type of groups you run and how frequently they are offered. In the next chapter I will look more closely at and offer some thinking about what it means to facilitate a group and what roles and functions the facilitators perform.

CHAPTER 2

Thinking about Facilitating a Group

As a mature student in the final year of a theology degree, I undertook to lead a group of fellow students who were in the years below me. We were to be a support group, offering each other accountability and encouragement during our journeys through the course and dealing with life issues along the way. I wince now and hang my head in shame at the mistakes I made. I knew about keeping boundaries and time in my head, but did not always put them into practice, neither was I good at allowing equal time for speaking. I grappled with emotional issues which should have been referred on to professional counsellors, which I was not at the time. In short, I was not a good facilitator, and the only thing I probably got right was that I cared for the people in my group and I think they knew this. I also think they were very gracious and forgiving. The issues I am going to raise in connection with facilitating a group are practical issues based mostly on what you can think about and do, before you learn the hard way.

A question someone asked me recently was, 'Who should run the bereavement group – volunteers or professionals?' It is undoubtedly more demanding to facilitate a group than to see an individual for an hour in a closed session in which they have the full time to themselves. So, initially if you are the professional tasked with setting up bereavement support groups, you may wish to run them with professionally trained people. However, it is my firm belief that well-trained and experienced volunteers can do an excellent job and save the time of the professionals too. Volunteers who are experienced bereavement support workers can be trained specifically in group facilitation. Training, plus experience, plus support, is vital for volunteers who are leading and facilitating groups. In one agency, the volunteers, who have already had years of practical experience of bereavement support, undertake six training sessions (three hours per session, making a total of eighteen hours) with experience of starting and ending their own group. They then sit in with an experienced facilitator for two groups, listening to the participants and the facilitator and contributing where they feel comfortable, so that they are part of the group and not tagged as 'observers'. After this they lead-facilitate a group with an experienced volunteer or a professional who monitors their leading. Once their lead-facilitating has been monitored and they have been carefully supervised, they are able then to fully function as facilitators on the team.

Some organizations do not use volunteers to facilitate groups because they think the responsibility for running groups should rest with the professionals in the organization. If you are the professional in the organization, it is certainly important that you retain responsibility for the group's progress as well as the safety and well-being of participants and facilitators.

If you are using volunteers, and you are certain of their competency and skills, you can also encourage them to do initial visits to prospective participants, as well as facilitate the groups. After each group it is vital to offer supervision to the facilitators, both professionals and volunteers alike, so they can debrief the emotions and difficulties of the session. In this way facilitators can deal with any problem areas or issues immediately, and if there are participants to contact or to visit in special circumstances then this can be dealt with appropriately. It is also a way of helping the supervisor know how the facilitators are working, and getting their immediate impressions of the group before too much processing has taken place.

When asked how many facilitators you need for a group, my first response is to say you need to think about the size of the group you have. For any group, of any size, I strongly recommend two facilitators at each session. But if the groups are larger than ten to twelve participants, you may have to rethink the way you run the group and involve more facilitators to cope with the numbers.

So, let's look at how many people should attend a group and how best to facilitate the number of participants. There are many discussions between those who run groups about this issue: some consider that a group of eighteen is feasible, some consider that a group of twelve is good and some believe that six to eight are worthwhile. You might well be constrained by the resources you have, and by how many people a room will accommodate. You will need to consider what your aims are and what numbers would suit those aims. If you are running a bigger group, it may be that you run it in two parts, the first part with some input and then dividing up into smaller break-away groups to discuss the issues. In this instance you need trained facilitators for each small group, and I would suggest two for every group.

One organization always runs their closed groups with two facilitators for a number between five and eight participants, because they are constrained by the size of the room. But they have also found that the size of the group can inhibit or encourage participation. The larger groups have not always been as successful for the quieter, more reserved participants as they did not feel confident enough to speak up in front of a larger number. On the other hand, the smaller groups have sometimes been intimidating for those same quieter people who wanted to just sit and think about what has been said and gain from others' input. The facilitation with at least two people is effective because while one facilitator is leading the discussion, the other can observe and support the lead-facilitator in handling the group dynamics.

Your style of leading and running the group will depend on the aims you have, the type of participant who has signed up and their expectations. Facilitators are not born, they are developed, and they may need to be developed in different ways for running different types of groups. In thinking through your aims, it would be important to think about the role of the facilitator as to whether they are there to assist the discussions, referee and time-keep and help bring in participants who are a little quiet; or whether the facilitators are to do any teaching or to give input, or are expected to operate in any other way.

WHAT MAKES A GOOD FACILITATOR AND CO-FACILITATOR?

In thinking through what makes a good facilitator, several faces have come to mind, and it set me thinking about what it is about them that makes them so effective. First and foremost I think they would say they are not experts in bereavement, though the group participants often want to place them in that role. A facilitator is someone with experience but someone who knows that every new group brings new challenges.

A good illustration is Dan, an experienced volunteer, who told me, 'I always come away from a group in awe of them [the bereaved participants]. They are amazing people and I always learn from them.' Dan has a humility that is part of what makes him a really good listener and facilitator.

While it may not be necessary to be a bereaved person in the same way as the group is, for example not being widowed if the group is for those who have lost a partner or a spouse, it will be necessary to have explored one's own bereavement issues before sitting with others who have been recently bereaved. There are often stories that will touch the heart and bring tears to the eyes of the facilitators as well as the participants. It is vital to have learnt how to cope with the tears of others without being hardened and cynical but also without being overly sensitive. This is an issue that faces all bereavement support workers, professionals as well as volunteers in the work we do. However, it can be even more daunting when faced with a group 'cry', and it is easy to be drawn into the sadness and the low mood of the group. A good facilitator will be sensitive to this but also not allow it to prevent them from maintaining the focus on what is good for the group. Being courageous and emotionally astute will help them move the group into reflective places.

To illustrate this, consider Linda, a volunteer facilitator, who is prone to her own low moods, and will often struggle to get a group out of the downward spiral into 'collective depression'. She has had to develop a way of empathizing that does not allow them to sink too deeply into despair. Linda has practised a way of coping that involves summarizing what is being said and then saying something like:

> 'What helps you get out of that place? Because you do – all of you have to get on with life at some point. So what is it that helps you move out of the sadness that can overwhelm you?'

In order for groups to work, the participants have to feel safe, in a place that is comfortable; moreover they need to be sure that if something threatened that comfort, the facilitator would be able to handle it. So the facilitator needs to be someone who can handle difficult situations without offending and without allowing the group to disintegrate. There needs to be an element of being able to bring things under control when necessary.

As an illustration, Joan was facilitating a first session of a new group, with one of the participants telling the story of what had happened in the hospital to his wife. Suddenly he was on his feet, shouting out his anger towards the doctors. The group was taken aback and a little perturbed. This man's anger had propelled him to his feet and he was reliving the scene. Joan was able to help the situation with some simple words that respected him and also reassured the group.

> 'Derrick, you're reliving the scene with the doctor and perhaps feeling some of the anger that you felt then towards him. It is a little scary for us to feel the energy behind those words as we experience your anger. I wonder if you are a little scared of it yourself?'

He sat down. 'I don't know what to do with it sometimes. It eats me up.' Joan helped move the new group through this awkward stage by saying, 'I wonder if others have had strong emotions that can sometimes feel overwhelming?' It was not an easy session, but the group was helped through Joan's quiet and calm way of dealing with the issue. Sadly, Derrick did not return to the group sessions as he felt talking about his grief would not help him, and he may have felt embarrassed at his outburst. He was offered individual sessions but also declined them. Sometimes people are not ready to face the hard emotions and need to be given the freedom to back away from what might be too frightening.

THE ROLE OF THE FACILITATOR

As we start to lead groups, we can feel as if we are apprentice jugglers, trying to keep many balls in the air and dropping some along the way, initially feeling awkward and inept. I have identified at least four aspects of the role of facilitator, which I outline here:

- There are the *practicalities* to consider.

- There are the *participants* to be mindful of.

- There is the *process* of the group and how it functions.

- There is the *subject matter* – what gets brought into the group for discussion.

All these aspects fall into the responsibility of group facilitation. Let's examine these aspects in more detail, and identify some of the 'balls' that need to be kept in the air.

Practicalities

The facilitator is responsible for setting up the group venue and ensuring all the practicalities are in place. This will apply to many physical things before the participants arrive. It might be wise to write yourself a checklist, so that you do not have to remember every detail every time a new group starts, but can refer back to your checklist. Here are a few things you might want on that list.

- **The group room:** If you are holding a group meeting and not a social event, you will need to make sure that the seating arrangement is as you want it, ensuring each one has their own space and can have eye contact with everyone else. You might need to decide which chairs you are going to use and whether they are suitable for all your participants, and if they are comfortable to sit on for over an hour.

- **The clock:** Check the clock is visible to the lead-facilitator.

- **Boxes of tissues:** These will need to be available to each participant, not necessarily a box each but placed so that everyone can reach one without too much effort if they need to.

- **Water:** Perhaps you need to decide if you are going to put a water jug out with glasses or plastic cups, and if you want a table in the middle of the circle for these things, or to the side, or not at all.

- **Refreshments:** If you are offering refreshments, the decision will be whether or not you have them at the beginning of the session, in the middle or at the end. Whatever decision is made, the facilitator will need to ensure that all is in place, with all the necessary ingredients to offer the refreshments as well as a source of hot water. If you have to liaise with kitchen staff, they will need to have your trolley or table set up in advance. It may mean the facilitator checking each time that it is going to be done – holidays and memos can mean your trolley might get missed one week, even if they have got it right previously. It can be awkward waiting for refreshments that do not arrive.

- **Handouts and information:** If you have handouts to give to your participants, you will need to have enough copies and have them in a place where you can lay your hands on them. If you have paperwork for them to complete (forms with the relevant information you may need to gather for your systems or for their security), you will need pens as well. You may wish to have a handout of the ground rules you are using (more of that later).

- **Attendance list:** For closed groups, a list of who is coming is helpful, to check if they are all present. If you have a reception area, it may be a good idea to give the receptionist a list so that they can see who is coming in and that they know they are legitimately present for the group, as a security measure.

- **Name labels:** For the first few sessions you may wish to provide name labels, as the participants may not be able to recall names even after several weeks of meeting together. You may want to ask them to put the name they *wish* to be known by on the label, as they may have a nickname or some other name they have chosen to go by that does not appear on your records. You may choose to write these labels in block capital letters yourself, as some people write so small that the object of doing it is defeated!

- **Flip chart and pens:** If you are writing up ground rules or any other notices, you may wish to use a flip chart as a simple means of communication.

- **Door notice:** Make sure, if you are in a busy part of a building, or in a room that might be booked by another group or department, that you remember to put a notice up on the door that tells people what is going on inside and the times of the group, if you think you might be disturbed.

The scouts' motto is the one we need to remember here: 'Be prepared.' The facilitators cannot leave anything to chance; they will need to arrive at least half an hour, if not 45 minutes, before the group starts to check all these things. You can guarantee that some early bird will arrive to throw you off track and distract you from your preparations. A word about clearing up after the group has left – if you were responsible for setting up a room in your organization, then you are probably responsible for clearing it away!

Participants

When everything is set up, you are free to give a warm welcome to the participants and to put them at their ease. The main consideration for your group work is of course your participants, so the facilitator's role is to make sure there is a comforting atmosphere for them to come into. Warm smiles and open handshakes go a long way to establishing a scene, and being taken care of so that people know where the toilet facilities are, and have time to use them if necessary. What you would expect to do for guests in your home is a guide for what you need to think of for your participants.

- **Setting the scene:** When you are ready to start it is the lead-facilitator's responsibility to get the participants to the right place and seated comfortably and to set the scene well for the group at the first meeting. Even though you may have talked to them about what the group is about and how it will function, you cannot expect they will have remembered, so the lead-facilitator will need to sketch out briefly for them what is going to happen and what their part is going to be in the group process.

- **Making the introductions:** You will need to have some way of introducing each other and breaking the ice.

- **Giving participants a voice:** Your role also requires that you allow people to have their say, when it is appropriate, and for a time-limited space. It may mean that you have to perform the role of a referee at times and blow the whistle on some who may be having more than their fair share of the air-space.

- **Allowing quiet participants to have their own space:** Your role will also be to allow people to say very little, if that is their wish. In practice, it would seem almost impossible for someone to come to a support group and say nothing, giving no details about themselves or their loved one. There have been occasions when someone has been so upset that they were not able to speak for some of the first session, not even able to say who it was who had died. But with sensitive handling and permission to be quiet, they are eventually able to talk. Dan recalls one participant who said very little throughout the time the group met, but who would be able at times to articulate what she had learnt and understood. Her final contribution at the end of the group was to say how much she had enjoyed it and how much she appreciated the others allowing her to be quiet. (More discussion is provided concerning silent behaviours in Chapter 4.)

- **Ensuring respect is given to all:** No one should be disrespected, so it will be the facilitator's responsibility to make sure difficult situations are handled and difficult or dominating behaviours confronted kindly. (More of this in Chapter 4.)

- **Modelling good listening behaviour:** People are not necessarily aware that they interrupt, talk over or disregard someone else's comments, so it is one of the functions of the facilitators to model this listening behaviour for the participants in order that it may become one of the norms for the group.

- **Enabling the participants to be independent:** Each one is responsible for themselves, and though we need to foster a climate of mutual support, it should also be one in which each participant takes responsibility for their own welfare.

Process

It is my experience that during the initial sessions of a group's life, there is a need to provide some form of routine, or structure, to facilitate the group's growth in trust and in the offering of mutual support. This will require the lead-facilitator to be active in the process of getting the group going and maintaining momentum. In order to do so there are factors to be considered.

- **Setting the boundaries:** You may wish to talk through what you could all agree to in order to maintain group safety. MacLeod (1998) writes about the difficulty that can be caused when there is a lack of guidelines or boundaries: 'the group does not evolve clear enough boundaries and norms, so that being in a group is experienced as risky rather than as a safe place to share feelings' (MacLeod 1998, p.321). Setting out the group norms or ground rules could be really important then. You will need to consider how you develop a more formal 'group agreement' to discuss such things as attendance, confidentiality, mutual respect and other issues. This can be quite critical for the health of the group, especially where a closed, time-limited group is concerned. Having a formal agreement means you can go back to it if necessary. To my way of thinking, any group needs to know how it is expected to function and what the limits are, and what is acceptable and what is not. (There will be more discussion of this throughout the book as it is such an important part of group functioning.)

- **Ensuring good time-keeping:** An essential part of respecting each other is respecting the time frames, so the facilitators are to model this behaviour for their participants. It is important to start on time and finish on time so that you show the importance of punctuality and respect for each other with time-keeping. During the group meeting or session it is also important to allow enough time for everyone who wants to speak, so helping participants to be aware that this is important.

- **Helping the conversation along:** The ability to use good listening skills is a major part of the role of the facilitators in being able to reflect what is being said and by paraphrasing and exploring the subjects with each participant. However, this cannot be done to the same extent as in individual work because of time constraints and the need to bring others into the discussion. Allowing for silences might, however, be another way of managing the group. Facilitators who jump in too quickly may prevent something worthwhile developing among the participants. It is being aware of and judging when the silence is either too long, or when it might be constructive. If the silence does become uncomfortable, the facilitator could ask for a volunteer to talk about what the silence might be for them.

- **Bringing people in who want to be heard:** There may be participants who would like to share but perhaps are a little nervous, or who are unable to join in because other participants are more vocal. It is important to help these participants to have their voice and to enable those who are a little tentative to try to give voice to their thoughts.

- **Making sure endings are well executed:** It will not feel satisfactory to the participants if the sessions continually come to an end by petering out or being cut off because time has run out. So the facilitator's responsibility is to establish a routine whereby endings are flagged up and everyone knows they have to be brief or that the session is going to come to an end.

- **Meeting the needs of the group:** This entails you as facilitator being able to assess the needs of the group and then facilitating the group towards meeting those needs. This is something that can be done in the group by periodically stopping the discussion and asking if there is a need to look at something specific or to do something different. So keep on checking with the participants that what they want to discuss is in fact being discussed. An ongoing assessment between the facilitators can be done outside the group.

- **Supporting versus helping:** In the support group process the facilitators are supporting and encouraging; they are not helping, in the sense of doing things for people. Their role is to enable the participants to do things for themselves, so, for example, rather than telephone a contact such as Age UK for them, the facilitator would supply the number for the participants to do it themselves.

Subject matter

You should consider what you are comfortable doing in groups. Some people prefer to operate without structured content, preferring to allow the group to take responsibility for the content and discussion matter, and some people prefer to have a set number of topics that are raised each week. This can be particularly helpful in a short, time-limited closed group where there is not a great amount of time to build up trust and relationships within the group. I must stress, however, that there is no right or wrong way of doing it, only preference. MacLeod (1998) writes:

> Some group facilitators utilize a high degree of structure in their groups, providing the group with exercises and tasks to promote exploration and growth... The other tradition is to offer very little structure, and for the facilitator to strive to create a group environment characterized by respect, empathy and congruence. (MacLeod 1998, p.318)

If you are offering a support group where you have certain topics for discussion, the lead-facilitation role will also be focused on the topic and leading the topic to some conclusions. (Further discussion of this and ideas for topics are discussed in Chapter 3.)

In my own experience, the subject matter raised in a bereavement support group is not always limited to the bereavement; sometimes it veers off into other areas. It is for the facilitator to assess where the conversation is going and whether something constructive for the whole group can come from it. It is not always an easy decision to make, but generally speaking the group will want to focus on the important things for them, and this can be the guide for the facilitator.

Here are some responsibility areas, in terms of the content, to consider when you are in the role of facilitator.

- **Redirecting the conversation:** At times, you might have to redirect the conversation back to the more important issues that have been passed over. The participants will not be listening with the same ears as you are, so they will not necessarily be aware of the importance of some issues. Taking them back to an important issue you have become aware of can be a good way of refocusing. If you have certain topics for the sessions, you may have to give quite a lead in focusing the participants towards that topic, as they may come into the group with another preoccupation and may not be focused on what you are discussing for the day.

- **Helping the group refrain from being judgemental or critical:** People come to groups with their own value judgements and prejudices and they might be tempted to be critical of another's way of coping or being. It is important to point out, very carefully, that each one has a valid way of thinking and being and we are not all made the same, so differences are to be welcomed and appreciated.

- **Sharing appropriately about self:** The participants will be curious about you as a person and what your experiences are, especially of bereavement. It is not my practice to share my own bereavement experiences (other than to acknowledge that I have had them), or indeed anything much of my own life story. What it is possible to share, however, is how something impacts you, for example when someone's story has touched you, or you are impressed by the way they have handled something. You can share your own thoughts and feelings at these points, so that the group hears something about what you are thinking and feeling.

- **Challenging inappropriate subject matter:** Sometimes you come across people who do not seem to have an awareness of what is appropriate and acceptable to share publicly, and for this reason the facilitator should be on the alert for inappropriate disclosure, for the safety of the other group participants. (More of this in Chapter 4.)

We have considered the role of the facilitator with regard to practicalities, the participants, the process and the subject matter. These are four of the aspects I identified in the role of facilitator, which I suggested command your attention. There is another aspect of the role of facilitation that needs to be addressed, which is about how to operate with two or more people facilitating a group and how to manage lead-facilitation and co-facilitation.

LEAD-FACILITATION AND CO-FACILITATION

For best practice purposes and for the safety of the facilitator and the group, I strongly recommend that there are at least two facilitators present at every group meeting. There is a protection for the facilitators in this, as they can talk over the issues after the group has gone and debrief each other. They can also share the burden of the pain and sorrow that is present in the room, and they are able to offer support to each other, as well as discussing what they might have done differently, what could have been said, and what needs to be addressed in the following session. Another factor is that there is protection for the participants, in the sense that there is another facilitator witnessing what might transpire and can be a buffer for them, if necessary. The facilitators are also witnesses to each other's words and actions so that, if there is any problem and any one of the participants brings an accusation against a facilitator, there is another side to it that can be submitted. A further consideration is that there are times when it comes down to an innate dislike of a personality or a personality type. While it might make fascinating work in a counselling therapy group to explore these issues, and prove constructive for the participant and the therapist, a bereavement support group is neither the time nor the place to do so. So, we may have to live with the fact that some participants may not appreciate us as much as we think they should. When there are two people facilitating, there are two personalities, and so the participants have an option, and we hope that they are able to accommodate at least one of the facilitators. In the event that they cannot, they usually absent themselves with some excuse or other.

There may also be times when one of the facilitators is not totally emotionally present and functioning at full strength and the co-facilitator may have to lead a little more explicitly than perhaps might have been the arrangement. An illustration of this follows.

Christine and Sue were facilitating a group which had not been easy to facilitate from the start, and in the early sessions it had proved to be quite a challenge for them. Christine was leading a particular session and had come into the group from a whirlwind of a weekend, feeling rushed as she entered the group. Sue became aware of the way Christine was floundering at one point during the check-in, when two of the participants began to question whether coming to the group was right for them and whether or not they should continue to attend. Sue could see that Christine was not fully aware of the implications of what was being presented, as she was still trying to facilitate the check-in. So, Sue gently suggested that before they continued with the check-in, or instead of it in fact, they might look at what was going on for these two participants. By intervening at this point for Christine, Sue was able to facilitate that discussion. This gave Christine time in which to settle herself into her role and into the discussion and fully come on board with facilitating the group.

It is possible that someone may leave the group in the middle of a discussion that proves to be too difficult for them, and it is at this time that a facilitator will need to leave the group to attend to the participant who is upset or angry. We hope that this does not happen, and it is wise for it to have been included in the ground rules concerning staying in the group even when it gets tough. However, we cannot always account for people's reactions and there may be the odd occasion when this does happen. If there is no other facilitator, there is no cover for the group.

It is for reasons such as those given above that I strongly consider it good practice always to have at least two facilitators in each group session. There are times, I understand, when it is not possible to have two facilitators, if an emergency arises. If only one facilitator is available, due to an emergency situation, like a hospital or doctor's appointment or admission, it would be advisable to discuss this with the group and negotiate what it means and what the options might be. (This situation could be something that is brought into a discussion on the ground rules at the first session.) The option might be to bring in another professional who might be available for that session only, or to cancel the session with a possibility of extending the sessions by adding another one later. In any event, the participants should be notified and there be a carefully thought-out decision. Some organizations will not go ahead with the session if one of the facilitators is not available. It is an important issue to discuss and perhaps even to have as a part of your group protocols.

I have found, however, that a group may be resilient to certain changes in facilitators when there are participants who are able to manage and who can adapt, but it can be disruptive for others if there is a change of facilitator or co-facilitator.

To illustrate this, several years ago we had an occasion when I was to lead-facilitate with Bob, a recently trained group facilitator. We had a good response for this group and there were ten participants. I was present for the first session and all went well, but during the following week my mother had a stroke and was in critical care, so I was suddenly unavailable. In my absence they did not want to cancel and let the ten participants down, so one of the most experienced volunteers offered to step in and lead with Bob. She did this for the group's second session, with the group's permission. But then the following week she had an accident and was unable to continue. Bob was now the only constant facilitator in this group. Fortunately one of the psychosocial team who was experienced in leading groups was available and offered to co-facilitate, with Bob taking the lead for a further six sessions. The group had been informed of this and had agreed, and happily the group performed well and was strong in their support of each other despite the disruption. It may also have been because they had some strong characters in the group who were able to take responsibility for themselves and wanted the group to work. I would not have planned it that way, and another group might not have worked as well. The alternative would have been to cancel the group, giving them another set of dates later in the year. It does show, however, that people can be resilient and resourceful even while enduring some of their worst experiences in life.

Different ways of joint facilitating

Let's take a further look at joint facilitation (I will address this as lead-facilitation and co-facilitation) as there are several ways of working with two facilitators: one way is for one facilitator to take the lead all the way through with contributions from the co-facilitator; another way is when the lead role is taken by each facilitator on alternate sessions; or a third way is that the number of sessions are divided into two and each one takes the lead for half of the time – that is, if there are eight sessions, each does four consecutive sessions, so that the one who starts does not finish the group.

A situation where one facilitator takes the lead in a group all the way through may be for training purposes, or also for the benefit of the co-facilitator to gain experience. Sometimes it can be the preference of one or both of the facilitators, as some people prefer to take the co-facilitation role and would not be comfortable taking the lead-facilitation role. Sometimes it depends on the personalities of the facilitators where one person is more comfortable with leading and does not wish to co-lead, so there needs to be an understanding between them that is workable for both parties, otherwise it may be necessary to change facilitators. Where there is to be one identified lead-facilitator throughout, they will take the lead in all the sessions, in the opening and closing of each session. This facilitator will be the one whom participants identify as the 'leader'. This does not mean, however, that the role of the co-facilitator is less significant than the role of lead-facilitator. The role of the co-facilitator is one that emphasizes the team nature of the work and provides support for the lead-facilitator. Below are some ways the co-facilitator can assist the working of the group.

- The co-facilitator can witness the different dynamics within the group. This is an important observational role, as the lead-facilitator will be busy with the process, concentrating on encouraging the participants to share and then listening to them. In witnessing and observing, the co-facilitator can assist the lead-facilitator where appropriate, by taking an active part in managing the dynamic they have observed.

- The co-facilitator can follow up on what participants say. The co-facilitator is the other pair of ears and eyes on the team and can bring other participants into the conversation where they sense someone has something to add to a discussion which might possibly have been missed by the lead-facilitator.

- The co-facilitator can share appropriately. It can be beneficial to have another person to call upon to offer some comments that might be helpful. The co-facilitator may refocus the group, they may change the direction altogether by their comments, or they may revisit something already talked about and offer some further insights.

- The co-facilitator can follow the lead-facilitator's train of thought and be congruent with what is being talked about. If they are following the discussion, processing and observing as well as allowing themselves to be in touch with their own feelings, they will be able to offer something of value that the lead-facilitator might not have had chance to process.

- The co-facilitator can support the lead-facilitator in non-verbal ways. In a practical sense, the co-facilitator probably needs to sit in a position so that they can have eye contact with the lead-facilitator in order to give non-verbal messages appropriately and discreetly.

In brief, the co-facilitator assists both the group and the lead-facilitator by actively listening, following, observing, processing, contributing and bringing in participants who might otherwise have been overlooked. It is an important role and quite demanding. In fact from my experience, the co-facilitator must actively involve themselves in the initial social greetings, and actively contribute in the process of the group interaction. If the co-facilitator does not do this, the participants may begin to feel distanced from them and may even start to mistrust them. When people do not share at some level, when their voice is not heard, they can affect the dynamic of the group in a negative way. The co-facilitator's role is certainly *not* a passive role and no one can afford to think, 'I'll just sit back and observe.'

When the facilitators alternate leading the sessions, the role of co-facilitator is a role that each one performs when they are not in the lead-facilitator's chair. There are some advantages to sharing the role of the lead-facilitator over the duration of the group. The participants learn to see the group as a shared one, and the one who started the group is not seen as the 'leader' but that this is an equal role shared by the two facilitators, so it avoids the implication that one is more senior than the other. The lead-facilitator of the first session can then view the group from the other side (literally and figuratively speaking) when in the co-facilitator's role. There is less pressure in this role to take full responsibility for the running of the group and so it allows the co-facilitator to bring in a different perspective when lead-facilitating the group in the next session. Being released from the pressure of leading means the co-facilitator can more easily observe the participants and the group dynamics, which can be helpful for reflection at the end of the session or it can help the co-facilitator come in with something during the group session.

LISTENING SKILLS

A personal conviction is that I would not consider asking someone to facilitate a bereavement support group who has not been through some training. I understand that there may be places of worship where pastorally minded people really care about bereaved people and some of those may have been bereaved themselves. It is still true to say, however, that if someone is identified as a good listener they would benefit even more from attending a listening skills course. The skills that are needed in a group setting are twofold: the listening skills we bring to support any one who is bereaved, and group management skills. The most important of the listening skills are the basic ones of active and reflective listening, clarifying and summarizing, as well as the exploration questions that open up the conversation for the person speaking. There are also skills that are needed for managing the group's flow of conversation. I shall endeavour to provide, briefly, some guidance as to the skills needed in the leading of a group. For this I have consulted the work of an American author, Alan D. Wolfelt (2004), who has worked with bereavement groups for many years and writes in a practical way about what is involved.

Active listening

Active listening is a way of listening that shows the group that you are following what they are saying. It may be a simple nod of the head, a smile in the appropriate place or an expression of concern when something difficult is being shared. Your non-verbal communication will show that you are attending to what they are saying. Your verbal communication might only be something simple too, like 'I see', 'Uh, uh', 'Mmm' or 'And then?' But be careful not to do this too often, as it can upset and even irritate people if you are too verbal. I recall this very well in a group I was attending as a trainee counsellor when I was told in no uncertain terms how another person felt about my 'verbal attending'. I have never forgotten how irritated he was with me.

Reflective listening

Some people refer to reflective listening as paraphrasing, but I like to think of it as acting like a mirror, reflecting back to the participant something of what they are saying, so that they are able to hear what they are saying and be encouraged to develop some further thought or share a feeling. We can reflect facts and feelings, both of which can be useful, especially when following the story of an illness or a death and you are trying to get it all in order, when the sequence of events can be helpful to understand. By reflecting the facts of a story (using a limited number of facts), the participant is then able to tell you if you are right in your understanding or they can correct you. Bear in mind it might be the way they have recounted their story that is confusing, rather than you who has confused the facts. Feelings are not always easy to talk about, and so if you are able to help the participants put names to their emotions it might be helpful for them.

For example, when listening to a story about a family of sons who did not do a great deal for their mother while her husband was dying nor have they done much since his death, you might say to her in the group:

> 'It sounds as if you bore the weight of the care for your husband before he died and are now perhaps feeling a little resentful of your sons who hadn't offered the support you'd have liked.'

She may find it helpful to have her feelings understood and named. She may even be able to say she is feeling quite angry towards them. Or she might be able to differentiate between what one or two have done and what the others have not done, rather than thinking of them all as one whole.

Reflecting is not easy to do as it can initially feel as if you are repeating back, so try not to sound like a parrot. Instead, try to hear what might be behind the words, and this is normally done by listening to the tone of voice and the energy with which things are said. Try to start with lower-level emotions, for example, 'feeling upset' rather than 'feeling angry', or 'feeling left out' rather than 'feeling abandoned'. There is power behind some words and they can feel quite loaded, so it is much more beneficial usually to start reflecting something lower down the scale than what you are hearing, and then the participant can develop it for you, if they choose to.

Clarifying

Clarifying is an important skill, because sometimes people can talk around an issue and not say exactly what they mean, and in so doing bring confusion into the conversation. It is helpful to be able to say, for example:

> 'I'm not sure I'm following, are you saying that you would like your family to be more supportive or are you asking that they stay away for a while?'

Or:

> 'I'm getting the impression that you have mixed feelings about the family's response to you, and you're not sure how you want them to react, is that right?'

Helping to bring clarity of thinking into the group means that others can also benefit from hearing what is meant and perhaps identify with the same issue.

Acknowledging others and bringing them in

It is helpful to be able to acknowledge the participants' body language or non-verbal agreement or disagreement. You might want to say, for example:

> 'While Tom was talking about his struggle to be alone at night, I could see a few of you nodding in agreement. I wonder, Carole, is that something you can relate to?'

Or:

> 'Tom, you seemed to disagree with Carole when she was talking about finding it easier to cope during the day. Would you be able to share what it's like for you?'

Helping others to think

When someone raises an issue that is troubling them, it can be helpful to ask the rest of the group to share their own experiences of a similar or different nature, so that they can collectively seek a way through. For example:

> 'Carole has been sharing about her way of coping in the day by keeping busy. How are others of you beginning to tackle the problem of managing your days?'

Observations

It may be helpful to make observations about the way participants are making some small adaptations. For example:

> 'Carole, I've noticed that you are more comfortable with sharing things in the group now than you were at the beginning.'

Or:

> 'Tom, it seems to me that you seem quite determined to make a few changes around the house, which might be something new for you.'

Focusing and redirecting

Sometimes there can be a lack of focus for a while as the participants settle into the group session, so it can be beneficial to offer them some direction. You might be able to take what has been said already and develop a theme out of it. For example:

> 'We've been talking about a few things this morning: the problem of managing the day; the loneliness you feel at night; and some of the practicalities of clearing out clothes. I wonder if we could develop it a bit further and think about some future strategies you might be able to take on board, to help you to start planning for the next few months, as the seasons are changing and the nights are drawing in.'

Or, you might consider that they need to focus on something more tangible, as they have been rambling. The issue of their own mortality is often not far away from their thinking, though it does not get raised necessarily, so if you want to raise it, this might be one way of doing it:

> 'We've talked a bit about this and that and we seem, if you don't mind my saying so, to be rambling a bit. I wonder if you would mind if I introduced something that we haven't talked about before. I would be interested in hearing what you think about...making plans for your own wills and funerals.'

(You can introduce any other topic, of course, in a similar way.)

Seeking mutual consensus

Sometimes a participant begins talking about an issue and it may be that it is not totally relevant for everyone. It could be useful to ask the group for their support for the issue to continue. You might say something like:

> 'I wonder if I could just come in here, Carole, and I know this is a relevant issue for you, but I'm aware that not everyone has the same kind of situation you have. So, I'm wondering if it is OK with you all if Carole talks about this right now, or maybe she needs to talk about it with one of us outside the group. What do others think?'

Leading

In addition to the above interventions, it can be important to remember that you can encourage the group to take responsibility for what they are to talk about, but at the same time you can help them in starting off the discussion by picking up on something one participant may have said and going back to it. For example:

> 'Jane, you mentioned earlier on that you haven't got a lot of energy at the moment and I wondered if that was something new for you, and if others are finding the same thing happening to them.'

Or you could have a poem or an extract from a book to read to them that you feel will help start the group conversation for the session. Do not be too perturbed if they briefly acknowledge your effort but do not take it up as you expect; they will take their conversations off in a direction that is relevant for them at the time.

Challenging

The word 'challenging' always seems to be a bit of a threat to us as facilitators; we struggle with the concept of offending or upsetting someone. Yet if a challenge or confrontation is done well, it can help the participant think through what they are feeling and saying. By challenge or confrontation I am not thinking of a bullish stand, or a 'Mexican stand-off'. I am thinking of ways of helping people see that they seem to be contradicting themselves, or are not seeing something that may be obvious. For example:

> 'Jane, you say you don't think you're coping very well, but you've told us about the ways you're spending your days which are very busy and you seem to be coping at a certain level. I wonder what it is you're expecting of yourself?'

Or:

> 'Bill, you've said a few times that you don't have support from the family, but you've also told us that your daughter is doing your shopping and your son is stopping by in the week after work, which seems to be quite supportive. I wonder what it is you would like them to do to be more supportive of you?'

Summarizing

Summarizing is quite a useful way of drawing the group to a close or when it is time to move on to another topic. Summarizing is not reeling off a long list of all the subjects that have been discussed. As a facilitator it might be useful to keep a mental track of the main topics the group has brought up and offer the topics back to them. In doing this they can see that something constructive has happened in the group and they can begin to understand the group process. So it might be helpful to say something like:

> 'It seems to have been a busy session, today. We've talked about some of the coping strategies you've had for keeping yourselves busy, as well as thinking about the support you've had from family members and others, and we've touched on what it has felt like to be going to functions on your own. Maybe next week, if it's still relevant (or maybe now, if you have time), you may wish to think about this a little more and how you cope with family events and socials when the family seems to make demands of you.'

The above skills are some of the main ones to have in place when listening and supporting in the group. In a group there is reduced air-space, as I have alluded to before. So the facilitators are not able to treat each person as if they are having a mini-support session. The eye, ear and focus of the facilitator must always be on the needs and the functioning of the group, even if this is at the expense of the individual's desire for time. Developing a balance in the ways of speaking with individuals and also managing the group is important.

We now turn our attention to some of the group management skills it is necessary to think about.

GROUP MANAGEMENT SKILLS

Having a structure or creating a routine

Whatever type of group you have set up, be it a social group, a more formal group or a drop-in group, there will need to be some kind of structure to the proceedings, or a routine established, and some modelling of the behaviour and group norms that are acceptable. It is not acceptable and not kind, for example, for people to gather in cliques and leave others feeling like outsiders trying to get in. It is not acceptable for everyone to talk over each other, interrupt or to hog the proceedings with their own stories; nor is it acceptable to dismiss someone else's feelings or ridicule how they are feeling or how they are coping. It may also not be acceptable for people to go in and out during the session, unless you have set it up that way.

Establishing boundaries

The group needs to have the boundaries and norms spelt out to them at the beginning and if necessary to be reminded of them in further meetings. Here are a series of questions I would suggest you think through so you can make a list of what you want to say about the way a group will function and the norms that will be set:

- What do you want to do about timing? Will it be important that they are on time?

- How will you deal with those who are early and those who are late?

- Do you want to ask them to let you know ahead of time if they might be delayed so that you can go ahead and the rest of the group can be informed, so no one worries about them? (This might be especially important for closed groups.)

- How many sessions or meetings do you think they should attend in order to get some benefit from the group?

- If they are away on holiday or have a hospital appointment at some time during the period of the group, how does that impact on the rest of the group and how will you cope with it? (Again, this is more relevant for closed groups.)

- What will happen if a facilitator is not able to make the group session? Does the group get cancelled or should it go ahead with another facilitator?

- How will the group feel about participants getting up to leave – distracting themselves and others?

- When participants get upset, how do they or you want other participants to respond? What can they expect from you, the facilitators, when this happens?

- How do you encourage them to share and be open with each other?

- How will you make sure that participants do not begin to chatter over you and to each other?

- How will you cope with hard-of-hearing participants? Or participants who are sight impaired?

- How do you want to start and end?

- What do you do about participants who are talking in a realistic way of ending their lives, or of suicidal thoughts?

- How does the group want to manage participants sharing their religious beliefs?

Establishing 'ground rules' might be an easy way of addressing some of these issues. There are several ways of handling ground rules. One way is to use a written set of rules that are easy prompts for the facilitators; another way is to allow the group to establish the rules for themselves with your guidance.

When using a pre-prepared set of rules, the facilitators can add in their own details about each point. (See Chapter 3 for an example of a pre-prepared set of ground rules.) It might be thoughtful, for those whose literacy skills are not so good or for those who might not be able to see very well, to say something like:

> 'We've come together from different experiences and backgrounds and you might never have been in a group like this before, and especially not for this reason. We like to set out a few guidelines that we hope you can all agree to. We call them "ground rules". These are written up on this handout. (They will all have been given the handout as we are talking.) Now, I hope I won't be offending any of you if I read these out and then talk a little bit about each point and answer any questions that might arise out of them.'

Usually the participants are quite agreeable to this, and each point is read out and then addressed, allowing for anything else to be added, for example about absences and how they can affect the group; about toilet visits or getting upset and staying inside the group; anything, in fact, that needs some clarification. Kindred and Kindred (2011) provide a brief overview of the subject of establishing group norms in a helpful chapter, 'Boundaries and Rules'.

You might be a little alarmed at raising the question of suicidal thoughts, but it can happen in a group, and so you have to think through how you will address it. This particular issue became a reality for one organization because of an incident in one group where someone began talking about suicide and nothing had been discussed about what would happen in such a case. As a result of this incident, it is now flagged up in their groups at the outset. It might sound alarmist or morbid to be bringing the idea of suicidal thoughts up at the initial meeting, but it is better to be open about this issue. If it is not addressed and someone starts talking about suicide, the other participants can become worried, probably distracted and fearful for themselves and the participant. If it has been clearly stated, they know the facilitator will be following the issue up with that particular participant.

As an illustration, I had a participant once who was talking in a way that was quite distressing for the other group members. Phil presented in a low mood and was clearly very down, and I observed that two or three times in the third session he turned the conversation to himself and his dark thoughts about 'ending it all'. I could see that other participants were looking at each other and then at me. I had to confront this in a practical and direct way so that they

knew I was managing this situation and following through with what
had been discussed at the initial session.

> I said, 'Phil, I'm concerned for you that life seems so bleak and that
> you get thoughts of wanting to end it. When we began our group
> sessions, I mentioned in the ground rules that if there were cause for
> concern for anyone's safety that we would need to raise it with them.
> I wonder if we might have a chat with you after the session, or if I
> could arrange to come to see you at another time outside the group.'
>
> I had got his attention, and he had got mine. He said, 'Oh it's
> nothing to worry about, I won't do anything to myself, if that's what
> you mean.'
>
> 'Well, Phil. It would be really good to chat about it outside the
> group, anyway.'
>
> Then turning to the group, I said, 'Phil has raised an issue of
> experiencing hard and dark days and nights. I wonder if others
> experience that same kind of dark despair.'
>
> (Nods of the head from a few.)
>
> 'Perhaps one or two of you might like to share what you do to cope
> with those times, and how you manage to get through them.'

The participants then, thankfully and with relief, I think, started to
talk about the practical things they do when they get 'down in the
dumps', as one participant put it. The mood lifted a little and they
were able to move through the 'dark' place Phil had taken us to. In
my discussion with Phil outside the group time, he said something
surprising: 'I wondered if you meant it at the time...when we started.
That's a hard thing to do, but you did it, and I want to thank you for
it – it showed you cared enough about me.' And he shook my hand.
Not for one moment do I think Phil got over his dark days, but he
spoke less about them, and the others knew that the issue had been
dealt with, so the group remained a safe place for them.

Having a set of pre-prepared ground rules is one way of handling
the situation; the other way, as previously mentioned, is to ask the
group to form their own ground rules. It might help to discuss the
questions I have listed above with the participants at the first session.
This is a democratic way of doing things, and involves people in
thinking about the way they want to run their own group, but it takes
time. You could have a list of the questions and a flip chart available
so that you can write down their suggested rules. This activity might

form the first session of your group, depending on the timing. If you are meeting for several hours, it could form the first part of the meeting followed by refreshments and then meeting back together to start your support work. I would suggest that people have some prior indication that you are going to do things in this way so that they do not arrive ready to start with their stories about how they are coping or not coping.

Initial sessions

At the initial sessions, it may be necessary to be a little more structured with the participants than you might otherwise be, until they are comfortable with the way things are going and they can be responsible for themselves (Dies 1983). The initial session may be quite nerve-racking for some participants, especially when they are faced with saying who has died and the circumstances around this. It has happened occasionally that someone has not been able to say the name of the deceased person, and it may help if the facilitator gives the details as they know them, saying something like:

> 'Jane, I wonder if it would be OK for me to give some details here for you as you seem quite upset at the moment. (Pause for her agreement.) Jane's husband, Harry, died of cancer in May.'

An alternative way of starting the first session would be to ask the participants to share, for a minute or two with a person sitting next to them, some specific things such as who it was that died, when and what of, and a little about their family. Once they are drawn back to the main group, each participant introduces the person they have been talking to. In this way the details are shared quietly with one person and then they are introducing someone else's details rather than their own.

Another way of starting the session is to ask them to explore what it is they are expecting from the group and what fears or concerns they have about attending the group. Again you may need to record these on a flip chart so that you can have them on the wall or bring them back at the end of the group. If you do not have space for a flip chart in your venue, then the co-facilitator can record them and perhaps have them typed up for later sessions. It is, without doubt, essential to think through how you will start the first session, which can be particularly poignant and painful for some.

Being structured does not mean you have to be directive, so participants can still bring up the issues they wish to discuss. However, in the first few sessions you might find yourself starting conversations off. For example:

> 'We seem to have had a general catching-up time so far in the meeting, so I was wondering if we could start getting to know a little bit more about each other's loved ones. Perhaps you would like to think about what made them special and what strengths they had that made others appreciate them, and what others would say about them.'

This might help to focus the conversation on something more specific once there has been a general chat about how they have been or how they have survived the week. As they progress, the participants will understand that they can initiate their own topics for discussion.

As an illustration, Sue was facilitating a group and, after they had all checked in, one participant said, 'I'd like to know what others have done with the ashes. I've got this problem with knowing what to do and the family seems divided on it. So what are you all doing? Or what have you done?' An exceptionally fruitful discussion ensued with all the participants telling her what they had done or were going to do and why. Because they had had experience of sharing their stories in a round, they stuck to that structure and went round without interrupting, with Sue asking questions as they went along. It was an example of how structuring and modelling can work well for the group's benefit.

When participants take responsibility and start to make suggestions or bring in different things, it feels as if they are taking ownership of the group and also of their own adaptive strategies.

An illustration of a participant who took some initiative that moved the group on was when Jenny, a widow attending one of our early groups, decided to bring along some photographs of her husband, saying, 'I've talked about Stan so much, I wanted you to see what he looked like. These are some snaps we took on a holiday in Spain when he was really well.' She went on to talk about their holidays and their shared interests, and the following week all the others brought in their photographs. It was a turning point in that particular group, and we have made a point of suggesting ever since that if they wished to they could bring one or two photographs in. Some people, of course, are not ready to handle the photographs, so we ensure that there is no pressure for these who find it hard. Sometimes, though, it is this group activity that helps them make that first step in being able to look through their photographs and put one or two out again at home.

Hanging topics

At the end of a session you might find that there are subjects left hanging and the time has run out for discussion. It is a strategy for using this discussion as an opener in the next meeting. So you can say something like:

> 'You know, Bill, we're coming towards the end of the session right now, but what you've raised is worth a bit more time. So rather than try to rush it now, perhaps we can come back to it in the next session, if you want to.'

It is wise to have a little notebook and pen with you, to write down these topics so that you do not forget to raise them at the next session. It may or may not be the topic that Bill wants to come back to, but you can offer him the opportunity and he can go with it or not. Sometimes participants have had an informal chat outside the group during the week and feel satisfied with that. On the other hand, it may be that Bill has been waiting to talk about it all week and you need to honour that and not disappoint him. So you can say something like:

> 'Last week, Bill raised an issue that sadly we didn't have enough time for. So I wondered, Bill, if you felt you would like to start today with that issue. If you've dealt with it during the week, perhaps you'd like to share how you did that.'

The invitation is there for him to take up or put down, but if he has resolved it, it might be of interest to the group as to how he managed it. This is, after all, part of the mutual help that participants get from sharing the group experience.

Keeping it going

At any time during the session the conversation may run dry, so it is a good idea to have some ideas up your sleeve. Rather than introducing something entirely new, it is preferable if you can go back to address something that has been mentioned or touched on in a previous session, so you know it is something relevant. In this way you have a strategy for keeping the group going. Some groups will not need your intervention in this way, as they have so much to talk about they do not reach a quiet patch. But some groups need a little more assistance. Keeping a log of what they have talked about at the end of each session and coming up with some ideas before you start the next session is good practice. Some of those ideas may be around practical issues, to help a group become more positive:

- What do you do to manage when you've gone out for the day and come back to an empty house?

- What have you found works for waking up at night and not being able to get back to sleep?

- How do you manage the family get-togethers when you don't feel like going, but they want you there?

Some ideas may be around the memory of the deceased person:

- What was your loved one's favourite...holiday, food, programme...etc.?

- What would your loved one be most proud of in their life?

- What were you most proud of in him/her?

Some ideas may be around their own adaptive strategies or of relearning their worlds:

- If you could project yourself five years forward from here, what do you think your five-year older self would have to say to this self? (Neimeyer 2011)

- Of the things you have had to cope with, what has surprised you the most in how you have coped?

Some of these ideas will work better than others, depending always on the group make-up, but for those groups where they fall quiet and the silence gets uncomfortable (remember this is not a therapy group), you will need to manage it. Groups vary in their levels of commitment and participation, as well as their levels of emotional intelligence and willingness to engage. They will need to be managed, and your skills will be tested even in the best of groups. In Chapter 4, I discuss some of the ways in which you can manage the more difficult behaviours, and in Chapter 5, I look at some of the pitfalls you can unwittingly fall into.

Record-keeping

You can assist the process of managing the group by keeping certain records and making sure your note-keeping supports your work. An example of a simple record is given in Appendix 3. This keeps a record of what is going on for the individual as they go through the process. Recording such things as covered in the suggested five areas below for each participant might be helpful as you track their journey in each session.

Questions to ask yourself about the participant

1. What emotional state did they appear to be in at the beginning of the session?

2. What issue(s) did they bring into the session?

3. What has been of significance to them in this session? (Was there anything new they left with?)

4. Who do they seem to be relating to in the session and why?

5. How did they leave emotionally?

You do not need to feel compelled to write up 'answers' to all these questions as they merely act as a guide for your reflection. In recording these simple observations, you will build up a picture of each participant so that, as you meet with them subsequently, you will have a history of the way they have interacted and what they have been coping with. As you continue to meet, you may be able to remind them of things they talked about and you may be able to observe, if possible and appropriate, how they may have changed. This is particularly useful in time-limited groups in the final session, where it might be possible to exchange thoughts about what people have observed about each other.

The final session

The final session of a closed group has to be handled in the same careful way as the first session; it is after all another goodbye, and it needs to be handled sensitively. Some groups do go on to meet by themselves and carry on the social networking, but as a group in this format and with you as a facilitator, it is their final session. A little planning will not go amiss beforehand with your facilitator and supervisor if possible. You might want to ask them some questions, and this might be what is suggested at the end of the penultimate session. For example, questions such as the following:

- In the group, what have you learned about yourself?

- What might you have learned about grieving from others here?

- Since coming to the group, in what ways have you made some adaptations and adjustments in your thinking, or your life?

- How might you have seen others in the group make some changes or make adjustments?

There is also the exercise I alluded to above, in which I use some observations I have made to give to each participant. I do not do the exercise with every group because it will depend on the way the group has worked together and how they have progressed. When I have done it, it has been received quite well, though some, it has to be said, take to it more than others. I will start by saying something like:

> 'This is our final session and we have met together over two months or more. We have been on a journey together and got to know each other a little better. I'm going to suggest that we do something that might seem a little risky to you, so I don't know if you're up for it. Let's see. During this time I've seen some things change and some things develop in you, and I'd like to share these with each one of you, and if you think you'd like to say something to each other, then have a go – it's not compulsory and no one will think any less of you if you don't.
> I'll start by saying to…(name)…'

I have talked through these observations before the session with the other facilitator and checked out what I say rings true for them too with regard to each participant. If we decide to share the role, we can take half the group each and give our observations alternately. This evens out the significance of the comments, so that the participants do not value the comments of one facilitator over those of the other. The comments are always something positive, definitely not negative, nor comments that can be taken as patronizing or judgemental. They need to be something simple but honest, something like:

> 'Jane, I've been touched by your courage in having to face some hard decisions.'

Or:

> 'Tom, I've really appreciated how you've shared yourself with us and I feel I've got to know something of the real struggles you've been dealing with.'

This needs careful handling and can be risky if you are not particularly used to working with groups, so it comes with a note of caution. Whatever you choose to do, it always helps to be prepared for the final session, as you might not want to use the time in a vague way. Although, it has to be said, be prepared for someone to throw you a curve ball, as illustrated in the following.

Linda and Dan were co-facilitating a group and had planned their strategy for the final session with some care, taking into account doing a review and a summing up of what the group had talked about over the last seven weeks. As soon as they had completed the check-in, however, Pam, who had been a relatively quiet participant throughout the sessions, started to talk about a serious situation she was facing that had just arisen. Most of the session was taken up with discussing this matter, and as she was quite distraught initially, the group all became involved and they made a collective choice to support her. The ending that Dan and Linda had planned had not been possible to implement. Sometimes these things happen beyond the control of the facilitators. Linda was able to make the comment to the group that this (the unplanned ending) reflects how life is for them in their bereavement; things happen that sometimes bowl them over and they have to manage. What was good for Pam was that she was able to bring it to the group and be supported by them in it.

Supervision

I have mentioned supervision at various times in talking about planning and debriefing. The importance of having someone outside the group who can listen to the process and the stories for the facilitators is of enormous benefit. There are questions a supervisor can ask of the facilitators that they might not have thought about or connections that the supervisor makes from the standpoint of another pair of eyes and ears. If the supervision can be done soon after each group session, the facilitators will benefit from not having to carry the group around with them for too long. Timely supervision means that current things can be addressed, rather than being left so that supervision becomes a historic recounting rather than an active engagement with the participants and their present journeys. Facilitating a group, managing the process and listening to the participants requires a lot from you, and you as a facilitator will need to feel supported.

In addition to the ongoing supervision of each session, the volunteers who facilitate support groups in our team also meet with me and the other facilitators after the group has completed its course. We all find these meetings to be of great benefit. At these sessions they have an opportunity to be reflective about the group as a whole, having had supervision spaced throughout the running of the group. Quite often things that have arisen in one group will inform our future practice, so we are able to rethink and revisit various practices and adapt our existing ones.

In this chapter we have examined some of the responsibilities involved in the role of facilitator; the practice of lead and co-facilitation; and some of the listening skills and management skills needed to assist a group in its functioning. In the next chapter we will look in detail at case studies of a closed and an open group, how they function and what some of the advantages and disadvantages might be, as well as some different types of groups that operate.

CHAPTER 3

Different Groups that Operate

If you have not facilitated a group before, you perhaps could do with a little insight into how it works and what you can say and what to do. So in this chapter I offer two fictional case studies based in practice, and a brief description of some other types of groups that run for bereaved people and have proved to be successful. The case studies are given for you to hear and visualize the participants and particularly the facilitators as they set the scene and establish their groups.

I will start with closed groups, because they are more defined and more structured than some other types of groups due to the shorter time of working and the focus that takes place during the process. No one imagines that over the period of the set time the group meets (whether it be two, three or four months) that there is going to be resolution for participants, or that they are going to be restored to their former normal lifestyle. Nothing will ever bring their normal life back again. This needs to be spelt out for them at the beginning, clearly stating that meeting in the group is only part of the picture and part of their journey.

In a closed group, after the recruitment stage, the bereaved participants come together and stay together for the duration of the group with no additions along the way. What follows is a picture of how one fictional group works in a hospice setting over an eight-week period, meeting weekly with two facilitators. Maggie is the co-ordinator, and four of these groups run in a year.

A CASE STUDY OF A CLOSED GROUP WITH NO FIXED AGENDA

Although the groups that run are closed groups, Maggie will often have a small waiting list so that if someone does not attend she can offer a place to someone else. In this way the closed nature of the group does not become effective until the group has perhaps been meeting for two sessions. They may wish to extend the group by a session, if this is feasible and agreeable to all. Maggie finds that this is a practical way of functioning that allows the group and facilitators to do what is right for the group in different circumstances.

Contacting people – preparing them for being in a group

Maggie's observation is that those who are already receiving some support often transition well into a group and are more prepared to share their stories and their struggles than those who have not received support and arrive at a group 'cold'. In an ideal world, Maggie would want all group participants to receive some support, even if it is simply a one-off visit from one of the support workers, before they join the group. However, in reality, this cannot always work, as some people send in their response slips indicating their interest in attending too close to the group's first meeting. She has a team of trained facilitators who are also experienced support workers; usually one of them is available to go out to visit the group participants beforehand.

Because they have limited space for group meetings, they run with a maximum of only six people with two facilitators in each group. Maggie explains:

> 'We operate groups four times a year, and so this means that we usually have just enough interest in each one. Occasionally we may run with only five participants, but if they're committed they'll stay the course and get a lot out of the social interaction and the intimacy of a small group. This of course depends on the people who're there and the way they interact with each other. The best of groups can gel really well and stay together long after the formal group has finished.'

Maggie believes in preparing the participants for the group experience by explaining what the group is and is not, as she thinks it is important they understand it is not a social group, but a place to focus on their bereavement issues. She explains the general structure of the time:

they meet for refreshments at the beginning of the group, which generally takes about a quarter of an hour, and then have an hour and a half for the meeting. The group does not have an agenda; each participant brings in what it is they have struggled with or what they wish to discuss, and time is allowed for that. This particular group is made up of people who are bereaved of a spouse or partner.

First session

At the first session Maggie always meets and greets the participants even when she is not facilitating a group, as they will all know her by name and will have spoken to her over the phone. During the time over their refreshments, on a label they write the name by which they wish to be known, which might be different from the one they use officially, and they are asked to complete a sheet of information for the hospice. This gets them doing something as well as having a drink so that they do not have to worry about trying to make small talk with strangers.

When they are all settled, she will do an introductory talk to the group before the facilitators begin. She says of this, 'I make no apology for repeating what I've already said to them over the phone, as I find they may not have remembered or fully appreciated what was said at that time. So I have a little script in my head.' Her script goes something like this:

> 'We want to formally welcome you to this support group. We appreciate that it might not have been easy for you to come today and you might be feeling quite nervous or apprehensive about what is to happen here. So, I'll go over a few things with you while you settle yourselves down.
>
> 'First, Jean and Dennis are here to facilitate the group for you over the next eight weeks, and they'll be going over a few things when I've gone, perhaps repeating a few things I've said, but also explaining what will happen so that you know what to expect. Today is a bit different from the way your group will normally run, as this is the first session. Jean and Dennis are experienced in leading support groups and so you're in good hands, but they won't be teaching you, or providing you with subjects, that's up to you. Though they may make a few suggestions if you run dry of things to talk about!

'You'll notice that there are tissues around the room; that's because we understand that there may be some tears in the meetings. We would encourage you to hold on in there and not rush out of the room if you start to fill up. We do acknowledge your grief is painful and want to be alongside you in it, though we can't take it away. There are no magic wands to wave and nothing we can give you to heal the pain you're going through. We just hope that by having time here in these meetings you'll be able to support each other and find comfort and strength from being in a similar place together.

'You're all here because you've lost a spouse or a partner and so there will hopefully be some similarities you find together. Sharing your experiences may be helpful to someone else. There may also be differences you experience and we hope that you can allow for each other to be in a different place or to think a different thing without being critical.

'We're not particularly offering you time to socialize, but a place to talk about what is happening for you and to talk about your loved ones, when others in your lives have moved on or want you to move on. But, if you would like to share phone numbers with each other outside the group so that you can meet up or phone each other during the week, then please do feel free to do so. There's no pressure to do that either. We want to encourage you to do what is right for you at this time.

'We would encourage you, though, to come to as many of the group sessions as possible as there are only eight of them. But, we do know sometimes appointments come up that you can't put off. Groups aren't for everyone, but we do know that, for some, the group can become like a lifeline at this time in their lives. I also just want to remind you of what I said to you all over the phone, that you might feel worse for a few days after the group, to begin with. From our experience this can begin to lift after a few sessions and people can begin to look forward to coming. So don't make a rash decision about coming to the group after the first session. If you do go through the first group and you don't think it's for you, please don't just stay away, give me a call to talk about it and we can possibly arrange for you to have alternative support. If this happens, then the group will change a little in shape according to who comes and who goes during the first couple of sessions. We realize that this can be a little unsettling, but we hope that you can accommodate some small changes at the beginning.

> 'Also, if you're going to be late or something comes up, we would appreciate you calling us to let us know, so that we don't sit here and worry about you or wait for you.
>
> 'It just remains for me to wish you well for this part of your journey, and I'll be back to see you in eight weeks' time to see how it's gone for you and to let you know what's available afterwards. In the meantime Jean and Dennis will be letting me know how it's going with you all, and hopefully I'll be supporting them while they're supporting you.'

Jean and Dennis then lead the first session with some opening introductions. They have already decided beforehand who is going to lead the first session, but thereafter, as a team, they have elected to lead-facilitate every other session. For the first session, Jean says she finds it helpful to have a postcard with pointers on it so that she can remember what to say so that nothing gets missed off. She asks them to introduce themselves with three things:

1. Who they are.

2. Where they are from.

3. Who it is that has died.

Jean explains to the group that she limits their introductions at this point to those three things so that everyone has a brief introduction before they establish how the group is going to function. She says to the group:

> 'I'm asking you to keep to those three things because we have some things to discuss as a group and, once that is done, we can go round again and get a little of your story from each of you so that at the end of the group we will know something of what has happened for each of you. Please don't be offended if I cut in on you at this point because this is only the beginning stages and you'll have more time to talk later.'

She and Dennis also introduce themselves after the participants with something like:

> 'My name is Jean and I come from… I have been volunteering at the hospice for fifteen years and facilitating groups for about ten of those years.'

Furthermore, Dennis says they might add, 'I have experienced various bereavements in my life.' He explains that they do not mention in the group if they have experienced the death of a spouse or partner, even if it is so, because they do not wish the focus to be on themselves, or to be questioned about that death or bereavement. Also, if one, or both, of the facilitators have not had that particular bereavement, they think it might distance the participants from them. But, by letting the participants know they have had bereavements, they are acknowledging that they are familiar with the bereavement process.

Once they have been round and they have given their information, Jean introduces the concept of the group process. She uses an analogy for it which she describes in this way:

> 'I think of what goes on in a support group in a word picture – a picture of you all coming to the table where there is a sumptuous dish of food. The only problem is you've been given very long-handled spoons to eat with and you can't get the end of the spoon to your mouth. So the only way you can eat is to dip your spoon into the dish and offer it to the person next to you.'

With this simple picture, Jean believes, they are able to get an idea of how the group will run. She then introduces the concept of ground rules. Jean prefers to use written rules that have been set out and have proved to be of help, and which have evolved over time. An example of pre-prepared ground rules is shown in Figure 3.1.

GROUND RULES

We need to feel safe in order to talk about what we have experienced and what we feel, especially after a bereavement when our emotions may be up and down and foreign even to ourselves. For this reason all groups of this kind agree to work within a set of ground rules.

1. Confidentiality

We need to feel confident that nothing we have said will be repeated outside of this room. We may not even want anyone to know we are coming to the group. So nothing that is shared by another group member is to be repeated outside the room and we don't talk in any way about other group members.

2. Respect

Different people respond differently to different situations, even more so in grief. We need to agree to respect each other's opinions even when we disagree. We also show respect in the following ways:

- **Don't use the collective 'we'.** Not everyone might be feeling or thinking what you are. Try to say, 'I feel...' or 'I think...'

- **No 'shoulds' or 'shouldn'ts'.** We don't tell others how they should feel or what they should think or do. Your family will do this for you!

- **We share time equally.** Sometimes when we are very upset or angry it can be hard to listen to others. In this group we all need time to talk and we all need to be listened to carefully. Only one person speaks at a time and we make sure everyone gets a chance to talk, if they want to. (If you feel you need more time to talk than sharing in a group allows, it may be more appropriate for you to have individual visits.)

- **We start and finish on time.** Punctuality is another way of respecting each other. If you know that you're going to be late or not able to make it at all, please try to contact us so that we can relay your apologies.

- **Mobile phones.** For the benefit of everyone, please can you make sure your phone is switched off? If you have a need to leave it on, please tell us beforehand.

If you share anything that gives us cause for concern for your own safety or that of someone else, we would need to raise this with you.

Figure 3.1 An example of pre-prepared ground rules for a closed group

Jean chooses to read out the ground rules, making additions and emphases as she goes along after she has read out each rule. She addresses the issue of confidentiality with a comment:

> 'I'm sure none of us would like to think that we're being talked about outside the group, and that we're the subject of gossip. If you meet outside the group or share lifts, it might be a temptation to discuss what is being talked about in the group, so it will be important to remember this simple rule.'

In respect to the concept of using the collective 'we', Jean says:

> 'There might be many times when you all share a feeling or a problem, but there will also be times when you don't. It would be really helpful to get into the habit of using "I" statements, rather than saying "We" – or making assumptions that you speak for the whole group. So when you talk about what you think or feel, just make a statement like "I feel…this or that."'

With regard to respect for one another's opinions, Jean adds:

> 'I'm sure you'll hear things you don't necessarily agree with and it is of course natural to have differences, but it will be part of our mutual respect towards each other to listen and not interrupt and then perhaps say what it is you feel about something.'

When Jean talks about 'shoulds' and 'shouldn'ts', she makes the comment:

> 'You may have friends and family telling you what they think you should or shouldn't be doing, so it would be good not to hear this here, where you're all in a place of struggling with something and trying to come to terms with different things. That also goes for musts and mustn'ts, by the way.'

The issue of air-space is quite an important one, so she says:

> 'It will be impossible to hear each other or to listen properly if you're all talking over one another, so I'm afraid I'll have to blow the whistle, metaphorically, if it happens. Please don't be offended if I have to say to you, "I'm sorry I'll have to stop you there, so and so is speaking and we all need to listen." It'll be my way of reminding you of the ground rules. I hope that will be OK for you all.'

Suicidal thoughts: you will notice in Figure 3.1 that the team has thought about how to address the question of participants expressing possible suicidal thoughts by putting in a statement of intent at the end of their ground rules.

After Jean has gone through the ground rules, she asks if there are any questions about them or any observations. She then asks for an agreement to a group 'contract' by saying:

> 'I wonder if we can all accept these rules as some simple guidelines to keep the group going so that we don't offend each other and so you can all get maximum benefit from the short time here with us. It will be like our group contract with each other. Can you all accept these as workable for you?' (Waits for agreement.) 'We won't be referring back to anything now, unless we have to, but Dennis and I may just remind you of the rules if we need to, like referees in a game of football or hockey. That's really our role here with you, to facilitate your discussions and encourage you as a group to support each other.'

After this Jean says to them:

> 'Towards the end of the time, we'll do what we call a "check-out" – asking you for a few words on how it has been for you today. This will be the pattern for the group sessions in the future too. And now you'll be glad to know, those are the formalities concluded, unless there are any questions... (Pause.) Perhaps we can start this part of the session by going round to hear a little more about what has happened for you and why you've come to the group. We'll be trying to allow everyone to speak so it will be time-limited. At this stage, perhaps we can let each one talk without being interrupted? Again, don't be offended if I interject and close you off, it's because time is more limited today. So who would like to start us off?'

Closing off the session

Jean has watched the clock as she steers the group towards the closure of the session, making sure that everyone has been able to talk. In this first session she has helped them keep to the topic, that is, what has happened to them and what has motivated them to come to the group. It has been one conversation with many voices, and they have been mostly respectful of each other, being helped by Jean's clear guidance. They have learned as they have gone round how to do it, so they have grown a little in confidence as they respond. When each one has concluded their story, Jean has summed it up and encouraged them to think about what they wanted from the group.

After they have all contributed, Jean says:

> 'Time has marched on and we're drawing to a close now. At the beginning I said we'd close out today with a "check-out". All that means is a few words of how this experience has been for you and how you are feeling *now* at the end of this session. Dennis will, I'm sure, help us out here by saying a few words about how it has been for him.'

Dennis is happy to oblige as a model for checking-out, and he says:

> 'I've been struck today by the way you've all shared so openly. This is really encouraging at the beginning of a group. I'm just aware that it has been painful and sometimes difficult to share so I hope you'll be able to take care of yourselves when you leave and be mindful of what Maggie said, that you might feel worse for a few days afterwards.'

Jean says:

> 'Thanks, Dennis. May I just remind you that a "check-out" is about closing the session and not about opening up another subject. So, I want to encourage you to share briefly now about the time we've spent together and how you think you're feeling as we finish today. Who would like to go first?'

After their check-out, Jean thanks them for coming, telling them that Dennis will lead next week's session and they hope to see them at the same time next week. She and Dennis stand and move towards the door so as to indicate the session is over, and they all take their cue to leave.

The content of the group

For the next six sessions the group meets and develops its identity, with participants being able to bring in subjects to talk about and learn from one another. They go through the stages of settling in and getting the measure of each other and the facilitators. They might bring in photographs and talk about their loved ones, and the ways they are coping or not, and the struggles they have.

Ending the group

At the end of the sixth session Jean and Dennis flag up the fact that they have two more sessions and ask the participants to think about how they would like to end their group and what they would like to talk about during the final two sessions. At the seventh session they again ask the participants to think about what they might do for their final session. There might be discussions around this, but generally it would be left for them to think about. They may wish to think about how they were when they started the group and what they have learnt from being in the group. They might just think about the 'niceties' though: one group suggested cream cakes as a way of finishing instead of the usual biscuits; another group suggested the participants go for a lunch together after their morning session.

At the beginning of the final session Jean and Dennis review the process with the participants. Dennis is lead-facilitating the group this session, and after their usual check-in, which focuses on the fact that it is the last session and how they are feeling about this, he begins by asking them what they might have decided to do for this session. They had not really brought in much by way of ending, so Dennis takes a lead:

> 'Would it be all right if I helped us on our way for today by summarizing what Jean and I have remembered about what has happened in the group for you? We seem to have been on a journey together over these past weeks, and it began with you telling your stories about your loved ones' illness and what had brought you to the group. Our next sessions covered the way you have coped after the death and funeral. Some of you have been involved in making specific complaints about the medical treatment in the hospital and you've shared those experiences with us. We had a thoughtful discussion about what to do with the ashes of your loved ones, as this is still an issue for some of you, and others were able to share what they'd done. Some of you have talked about how your families have reacted in different ways to what you'd have expected them to, and how that has impacted you. You've looked at photographs and talked about your relationships with your loved ones. You've been able to remember their lives and achievements and thought about the legacies they've left you all.

'Perhaps today we could look at how useful the group has been for you and we wondered if you felt you'd be able to say how you've experienced the group and in what ways you might have felt supported by it.'

This session is about reviewing where they have been as a group. Some are able to say the best thing about it has been coming and sharing, hearing how others have responded to their grief and situations. Some have been helped by the discussion about the ashes, and some really enjoyed talking about their spouses and partners and remembering the good times. They then move on to thinking about what the future might hold for them. A brief discussion follows about some of the plans they have for the next few weeks. Some say what they will take away from the group and put into practice.

At this final session, Maggie comes back to talk to the group and close off the final session. She tells them she will be sending out an evaluation form for them to complete, so that the hospice can go on to improve the way groups are run. She then says if they feel they could do with further support, they can contact her at the hospice: she stresses, however, that they should probably give themselves a month or two so they can have a more realistic picture of how they are coping. At first they may find they miss the group and they need to find something to put in its place. She thanks Jean and Dennis on behalf of the participants, and with these final words of encouragement the group closes.

What next?

What is next for these people – a social group, ongoing group or closure? What do the participants do after they have been to a closed group for a certain number of sessions? Some will want to continue and some will be glad it has come to an end. In a group that finished a number of years ago, Maggie was asked, 'What will we do now on a Thursday morning?' Her response was:

'What do you want to do? You've got some options, it seems to me. You can say goodbyes now and not worry about carrying on, or you can agree to meet every now and then, or some of you may want to make friendships that will continue. It's really up to you. But it will take organizing and it will take willingness from you all to keep going, otherwise it will peter out, when it's served its purpose.'

This group has gone on to meet on Thursday mornings – at least some combination of the group – and they have gone on holidays together and phone each other regularly. One of the options Maggie and her team tried a number of years ago was to allow people in the group, who wished to do so, to attend a second group, as well as bringing in new people who had not attended a group before. So, they had new people joining, along with some of the existing group, which made up quite a large group of people. They were trying this out as an experiment but were willing to be ruthlessly honest with each other about the outcomes. They saw the existing group participants offer a warm welcome to new participants, but they could see from early on there were cliques starting to form. It seemed one or two of the new participants thought it was difficult to share with the others and also felt that they were on the fringe of the group. Others felt that they were at a disadvantage to those who were more familiar with the facilitators and the process. The decision was not to continue with that experiment and to go back to offering one group only. Maggie says:

'I guess we were trying to bridge the gap between an open group and a closed group, but because it was neither one thing nor the other it did not work very satisfactorily. I do not regret trying to resolve issues in this experimental way, as I do believe it is a way of finding what does work and what doesn't.'

(There are some further ideas for answering the 'What next?' question discussed later in the chapter.)

Advantages of a closed group

The advantages of a closed group include the following:

- Dates can be fixed in the calendar and you can advertise ahead, so that people know the time frames that are in place.

- Your facilitators, who may be volunteers, are able to block off a certain number of dates in advance and are not kept going for months or years on end.

- If the group does not gel and is not a very cohesive one, there are only a certain number of sessions to be endured!

- Having a time limit does focus the discussions for the participants, especially when the final two or three sessions are in view, and people can be reminded of this and asked to think about what they might like to talk about in those sessions.

- Once the group closes, the facilitators know who they are dealing with and there are no more additions as they go along, so the beginning can often be a real beginning and people all start in the same place with the introductions, group ground rules and established norms.

- Although not always the case, there is probably less time for cliques to be formed in a closed, time-limited group.

Disadvantages of a closed group

The disadvantages of a closed group include the following:

- Your group may be smaller than you would otherwise have liked it to be if prospective participants cannot make the dates you have set.

- Some participants might not be able to make all the sessions as appointments come up or they may have offers of going away with family or friends. This means the dynamics change over the weeks, which are limited in the first place, with different people coming and going. Participants who have been consistent in attendance can feel disrupted by the changes and perhaps cheated of the full group participation.

- For those who came looking for friendship, it could be a disappointment if they have not found a kindred spirit in the group. You are limited to the people who originally join the group and so there is no opportunity of introducing new faces.

CLOSED GROUPS WITH STRUCTURED CONTENT

We have seen how a closed group that has no fixed agenda can function, and examined some of the advantages and disadvantages. Now we look at how closed groups that have structured content can work.

Some closed groups work with a more didactic purpose, that is, they introduce topics for each session with a short talk, a DVD or some other input, and then open up the group discussion with the same emphasis. The discussion of the material or the topic for the day might be done in smaller-sized subgroups if the original group started with a large number. The explanation of the ground rules and the way the groups operate can be done 'from the front' in the large group before splitting off into smaller groups. The personal introductions can be made in the smaller subgroups led by the facilitators. If it is already a small group, then after the welcome and 'talk', the ground rules can be established followed by the personal introductions. The facilitators may have pre-set questions, based on the talk given for the session, in order to start the discussions going. The feedback from these groups is often that they benefit most from talking together, so it would be advisable to leave most of the time available for the group interactions.

The subject matter for groups of this kind can vary, again depending on the materials available and the skills or philosophy of the leaders or speakers (if they are not the same people as the facilitators).

Some suggested topics for these groups:

- What grief can be like. Exploring your own grief and the struggles you face.

- Exploring the grief of other family members and the impact on you.

- Looking at the relationship you have lost (including sharing of photographs).

- Experiencing the roller coaster of emotions.

- Coping with relearning your world.

- Strategies for living alone.

- Strategies for dealing with anniversaries and holidays.

- Ways forward for the future.

- Other people's testimonies.

At some point, towards the end of the group sessions, it might be beneficial to have one or two people who have been bereaved for some time and are able to speak about their experience come to address the group about their own journey and how they 'survived'. It would be important to know the type of death and the relationships in the group so as to accommodate most people's situations. With the death of a partner or spouse, it might be ideal to have a mix of testimonies from one or two who have stayed widowed and not remarried, and one or two who have remarried, so that there is hope for both groups of people. It might be the case that there are participants whose last thought would be to enter into another relationship; at the same time there may be participants who have already begun to think about this and may feel guilty for doing so, and could benefit from hearing from those for whom it has been a reality.

Groups like this can be run in the day or in the evening, but this style of group meeting can also lend itself to a day's 'workshop' at a weekend. I would recommend that you bring on board enough trained facilitators to cope with a day's event. If you can accommodate it, resources-wise, you should think about having a trained children's worker with additional support workers who could work with the children of the parents you have in the adult groups. This would be to provide a programme of activities based around addressing the children's grief. Without this option you may be eliminating a number of younger bereaved adults with children, as they often do not have people to do their child-minding for them at the weekend.

Although it could be more demanding of our time, effort and preparation to set in place a structured workshop or weekly session, it might draw those people who do not feel able to enter into the less structured groups that operate without an agenda. The very nature of closed groups can be more intimate in the personal sharing but can also be more threatening to some. There is also the question of what you call the group. You might want to adopt the words 'course' or 'programme' alongside the idea of a support group: for example, 'A Bereavement Support Group – An Eight-Week Programme' and then list the topics covered; or, 'A Bereavement Support Group – A Twelve-Week Course for Survival'.

An example of programmes for bereaved people is the work done in Canada by Dr Bill Webster, who is a grief counsellor, author, TV host and international speaker on grief and bereavement. He operates from the Centre for the Grief Journey and runs the 'Community Grief Support Programme'. His website provides downloadable resources, information about grief and bereavement, and meditations. The programmes have been delivered in Canada since the 1990s and are run for people in the community. They provide a structured format which combines education as well as discussion, and usually run with quite large numbers. There is no screening process or assessments done, and they are led by trained facilitators. The programme lasts for six to eight sessions and the group becomes closed after the second session. Participants are allowed to attend the programme more than once. Some of the sessions include the following: grief as an emotional response to loss; guilt and anger; and adjusting to life after loss, including coping with loneliness (Betley 2011). I have listed his website in the Useful Resources at the end of the book.

A CASE STUDY OF AN OPEN GROUP

Having looked at a case study of a closed group that operates without agendas and having discussed closed groups that offer structured content, let's now look at how differently an open group operates.

An open group is open in the sense that participants can come and go; there is no specific finishing date as the group continues to meet and has a roll-over of participants, some of whom may not come for a while and then opt back in when faced with a new challenge in their lives. In the case study below, John currently facilitates two ongoing, open groups at a bereavement agency that supports the local community. He had inherited the groups from a previous counselling practitioner. There are usually between six and twelve participants at each session in both groups. This case study provides an honest and helpful review of the open group, and in it John also highlights things that can happen when people have been meeting for a length of time and feel familiar with what they have created. (Some further discussion on this issue appears in Chapter 5.)

Contacting people – preparing them for being in a group

People who have been bereaved can self-refer by contacting the agency, which is advertised widely through doctors' surgeries, hospital outpatient clinics, libraries, local council offices, funeral directors, places of worship, nursing and residential homes and such like. People who are interested in receiving support are given a phone number to contact. There is no definite recruitment and selection process, but after the initial referral has come into the agency office and details have been taken by the administrator, the prospective client is sent information about individual as well as group support, and people are encouraged to contact the agency before attending a group. However, the information also states that John will follow up with a phone call about a week later. The idea is that the person has had a chance to read through the communication and share their thoughts with other family members. When John contacts them, they have usually decided for themselves what, if anything, they would like to take up. If through talking to them he feels they have made an inappropriate decision, he discusses this, but it rarely happens. He says that people often surprise him by choosing a group when he thought they would prefer individual support.

The agency will take people on in their groups at any particular time after the death, and so the groups tend to have some who are in early grief and some who are a few years on. (Chapter 2 included a discussion concerning the length of time from the death to attending a group: people in the early months of grief may not benefit as much by attending a group as they might when they are a few more months on in their grief.)

John has identified that the vast majority of group participants over the years have been bereaved of a spouse or a partner. He also acknowledges that a frequent reason for the bereaved person to opt for the group is loneliness and wanting to meet others in similar situations in order to feel reassured that they are handling things as they 'should' be (their perception) and to feel a sense of belonging. As he may well have spoken to any new participant before their arrival, he is usually assured that he knows who to expect. However, John says there is still an element of the group being held on a 'drop-in' basis as someone may come without warning, and also there is no expectation of people having to give apologies for non-attendance.

The groups meet twice a month, but people can come to one or other or both. The sessions are 3.30–5.30 p.m. and 7.00–9.00 p.m. John asks for feedback when people have stopped coming, and one person said that he thought one and a half hours would be better than two. John put this idea to the existing participants and found that they unanimously voted to keep the timing as it was. He had also considered making the afternoon group half an hour earlier because some people were finding the 5.30 p.m. finish difficult in the winter due to getting public transport and returning home to an empty house in the dark. As can happen in long-standing groups, they had been accustomed to the times and they resisted any change when he offered them the choice. It is a point to bear in mind that the group is for the participants, and accepting their decision-making on such issues, whenever it is feasible and practicable to do so, enables them to take ownership of the group, though it may sometimes go against your own wishes.

The venue is a comfortable room with easy chairs. Free refreshments, brought in on a trolley, are served on arrival and this has the effect of breaking the ice as well as giving everyone a chance to arrive.

First session for a newcomer

John himself facilitates the groups but he always has a trained volunteer with him who can look after the group while he is greeting any newcomers. If he knows someone is coming alone for the first time, he will offer to meet them in the reception area. Also, the volunteer is there as a back-up should anyone want to leave the room, so that the group is not left alone. It is also good to have someone to debrief with afterwards. If John is on holiday, sometimes a colleague will cover and sometimes a second volunteer will be called in, which depends on the confidence of the volunteers. (Please note here that it may be necessary to consider how much responsibility is given to volunteers in facilitating the group, particularly when the main qualified facilitator is absent, which is likely to happen in an ongoing group at some time. It should be remembered that the volunteers need to be highly skilled, well supported and supervised.)

In terms of structure, John has an outline of how the groups work: there is a welcome and introductions for new people, and then an opening up to the group for their input. When he thinks everyone has arrived and settled, he starts the group off by welcoming everyone, and if there is someone new he goes over the ground rules and does introductions. For this, he asks everyone to go round and state briefly who it was that died and when. If they are too upset to give their introductions, John will offer to do it in order to give a context to the losses in the room. Then he usually says something like:

> 'So, has anyone got anything they'd like to share about how the last few weeks have been for them?'

John finds this is usually enough to get the conversation going. He thinks the groups seem to go better on the occasions when he says the least, as that is when the participants are really responding to each other instead of coming back 'through the chair'. However, he does keep a close eye on whether anyone is dominating and will try to bring the quieter ones in with a direct question if he feels they are not getting a chance to talk and share appropriately. 'Everyone will take a turn at some point, but inevitably,' he says reflectively, 'there are those who like the sound of their own voice rather more than others!'

The group's ground rules are printed on the group flyer, which they will have had in their original information pack, and copies of which are always available at the group. An example of an open group flyer is shown in Figure 3.2.

As the flyer contains the dates for the full year, existing ongoing clients will be given a new one in the autumn for the following year, so this is a good opportunity to review the ground rules. According to who is there, John may choose to emphasize one rule in particular, for example allowing everyone their share of the air-time, or respecting that they all grieve differently. John says:

> 'As I've alluded to, some people may be inclined to dominate. It's not easy. Interestingly, it seems that the existing participants understand the need of newer ones to take more time in their first couple of sessions, once they've found their voice. We have sometimes had conversations where a new participant has suddenly said, "Oh, I think I'm taking too much time." Others have then come in with, "It's OK, we've all been there – your need is greater at the moment."'

BEREAVEMENT SUPPORT GROUP

The purpose of the Support Group is to give people the opportunity to meet others who have had a bereavement and be able to talk in a warm and caring environment supported by experienced bereavement volunteers. There would also be an opportunity to talk on a one-to-one basis if you feel you would like to do so.

On your first visit you will be asked to complete a form requesting your contact details. This will only be used if we need to contact you regarding the Support Group meetings.

Guidelines for the Support Group

- Each member's situation is respected. What is right for one person may not be right for another.

- Each member is encouraged to participate in the group if he/she wishes, but there is no pressure to do so.

- Members of the group listen and support each other without criticizing or making judgements.

- All information about members and discussions within the group are kept confidential.

- The facilitator will not disclose any details discussed to anyone else unless they are seriously concerned for your safety or the safety of others.

Bereavement Support Group meetings will be held on Tuesday afternoons or Thursday evenings on the following dates and times:

Tuesday 3.30 p.m. – 5.30 p.m.	Thursday 7.00 p.m. – 9.00 p.m.

Refreshments of tea, coffee and biscuits will be served. Please be assured you will be given a warm welcome if you decide to attend.

Contact details:

Figure 3.2 An example of an open group flyer including ground rules

A problem arose once, though, when John was away, and there was apparently an uncomfortable situation where a new participant talked at great length about his wife's illness. The group at first seemed to accommodate this as they knew he would need time to talk about his experience. But unfortunately he continued to tell stories of his whole family's lives, and at this point another participant suggested it was not really helpful to hear all this as they were there to discuss their own bereavements. The new participant left the group at the end without saying anything to anyone. On his return John did some investigating, and also talked to the two facilitators who led the session. John was able to help them understand that the group participants are all adults and responsible for themselves, all with a right to an opinion. He feels that firmer control at some point would have been helpful, but he admits that situations like this are part of the challenges that face us when facilitating groups. The participant was contacted and offered individual support, though as you might expect, he declined it.

In an ongoing, open group an important question to ask is: How do you enable participants to move on so that they are not with the group for years and become dependent on the group or become a hindrance to others' growth? John relates that one person in the afternoon group had been coming for five years, and some for two or three. They needed to move on. John says, 'I tried to suggest that if they wanted a social group they could arrange one, but there wasn't really anyone willing to take the initiative.' John has eventually been able to signpost these people on to other more social-based groups in the community.

While we might be concerned at the idea of someone being in a group for five years, there are times when some people may benefit from being part of an open group for a good length of time, and it might be significant in the adjustment to their loss that they are not hurried out of the group.

John tells the story of Jim, a man who had been coming to the group for about two and a half years:

> 'Jim was in a very low state for about the first year. He suffered terribly with depression and was desperately lonely. Then after about his first year, a woman joined who had lost her husband and was left with young children to bring up. Her story really seemed to touch

Jim and he was really caring with her. The woman went through some really difficult times and was trying to keep going with her busy job while fitting in the demands of a growing family. She eventually started to feel more able to cope and stopped coming for a while, but Jim always asked after her. The start of Jim's own recovery soon followed. I always felt that he thought if she could make it, given her difficult situation, then he could too. At a later session Jim told new participants, "This group has been a real support to me – I was in a terrible state when I first came. Hang on in there; you can make it, even if it doesn't feel like it right now." Jim's presence in the group was of value to the whole group. It was right for him to take that amount of time, but he was also helped soon after to move on from the group.'

Then there is the story of Mike, who had been with the group for about eighteen months. He had been a carer for his late wife over many years. He was grateful for having been allowed to stay with the group over this length of time, acknowledging how much it had helped him to talk to others, which had taken him time to learn to do.

John is very conscious of the issue about allowing some participants to attend the group for a long time, but there are others who have a shorter time in the group. Having heard about various websites or other groups, they have become involved in social activities and events that are more appropriate to their age and their circumstances.

This is a brief but honest assessment of an open group, raising some of the issues that might be met along the way.

Advantages of an open group

Here is a summary of some of the advantages of an open group:

- A positive advantage of an ongoing, open group is that the participants are able to get to know each other well and possibly find that they form some good friendships over the time they are in the group.

- There can be a core of participants who keep the group going and are able to welcome others into the group, and in so doing they are able to have fresh impetus and the group need not become stale or fixed.

- The new participants into the group can be assured of a way forward as they identify with participants who have gone through some of the issues ahead of them.

- There can also be a longer time allowed for healing and growth to take place and so participants need not feel constrained by a time factor.

- As the time from the death of their loved one moves on, new issues can be brought into the group as they experience different feelings and different life events. They may go through anniversaries of birthdays, wedding anniversaries, the beginning of the illness, or recalling what was done a year ago, as well as the anniversary of the death.

- As new participants join the group in ones and twos, rather than a whole group starting all over again, the facilitators have time to assimilate the new stories.

Disadvantages of an open group

Here is a summary of the disadvantages of an open group:

- A disadvantage in facilitating such a group is that you have to work really hard at making sure the participants do not stay for years without a real need or a good reason.

- One of the main concerns for any long-term, open-ended group is that participants can form dependent relationships that may not be helpful in the longer term for them.

- A familiarity between the facilitators and the participants may develop that perhaps prevents some good work taking place, no matter how the facilitators try to keep a professional detachment.

- If not carefully handled, the group can also become a social group without much of an aim. It could be difficult to keep the group focused if you want to provide a supportive, self-help environment with more emphasis on the therapeutic value of a group.

- There is a risk that a few dominant characters who have attended the group for a while may outlast many others who vote with their feet as a result of feeling excluded. It is hard work ensuring that this does not happen.

- In the same way, you may find cliques happening between those who have found comfortable friendships and camaraderie so that new participants find it hard to feel welcomed and might struggle to feel there is a place for them.

- After a while it may be that issues are being repeated and participants are going round in circles discussing the same struggles they had a few months back, without making much effort to resolve them.

- If you have people who are still struggling with their grief in an intense way, a year or so after the death, it may not be helpful for new participants to see, as they may feel there is not much hope for them.

- In the same way, those who have been in a group for a while may experience a throwback to the times they experienced great sorrow, when they hear the stories and pain of new participants, thus undoing any progress they feel they might have been making in adjusting and adapting to their new situation.

The incident occurring when John was absent (described earlier in the case study) highlights the difficulties in maintaining the continuity of facilitators in an ongoing group when there are holidays and absences to be taken into account. Some group facilitators may choose to negotiate with the group ahead of time, in order to postpone those meetings when the usual facilitators are not available. (It may be advisable to have a discussion on the ground rules for such occasions and already have a plan in hand.) If meetings are postponed, it may cause concern about people who turn up without having contacted the facilitators ahead of time. Whichever route you take, it still poses some questions for both facilitators and participants, but with planning, these issues are not insurmountable.

The incident when John was absent also raises the issue about whether or not people should be prepared for the group, or whether people should be assessed ahead of time for their suitability and their needs. The incident also raises the issue of having suitably skilled facilitators who might have been able to divert the participant and change the direction of the group.

OTHER GROUPS

Closed groups and open groups are two types of support groups that run and usually have the aims of focusing on the mutual support that can be gained by sharing experiences in a group. There are, though, other groups running that are worth special mention. I will briefly discuss some of these below, including social groups, special focus groups, walking groups, online bereavement support groups and creative groups.

Social groups

A question that can come after a closed group has run for several months, as I discussed earlier in the chapter, is what to do next, as the participants may not feel they have completed what they wanted to do. Cruse Bereavement Care, a national organization in the UK (see Useful Resources at the end of the book), has a 'Friendship Group' for those people who meet any of the following criteria: they have finished a closed group; they have finished with individual support; or they have been assessed as being able to have this kind of activity, without receiving any previous support. These people can go to something more social, for the contacts and activities as well as for fundraising efforts, which provides those who attend with a purpose and a focus. The group runs under the supervision of trained bereavement volunteers who are responsible to the local branch committee. The group may meet in a designated hall, a meeting place, a local facility or a restaurant or pub, depending on the organized activity.

Special focus groups

In Chapter 2 we discussed people who are bereaved by different kinds of deaths and different relationships being placed in one group. It was considered that it can be done providing there are several ways to accommodate their needs and with specific input from the beginning. However, there are some groups of people who might find it more beneficial to be in a group where people have been bereaved by the same kind of death, for example those experiencing a stillborn baby or the death of a very young child. The special focus of this group would be on the fact that the child had not been able to live and develop and so there are few, if any, stories or relationships to hold on to. There are also those people bereaved by suicide, or as a result of a murder, who may find themselves in difficult circumstances, initially because of the involvement of other agencies such as the police, the judicial system as well as possibly social services. Because of this, some bereavement organizations have run special focus groups.

Groups for those bereaved by suicide or murder can beneficially run on a drop-in, open basis, to allow more flexibility for its participants who might need a longer time to deal with their issues than a closed group would offer. Because of the intensity of activity around different stages of the investigations and proceedings, participants may feel the need to attend at different times: for example there may be more frequent attendance during the time leading up to the inquest or even after it. The scene of a suicide as well as a murder automatically becomes a crime scene so that, if the suicide or murder was in the family home, the home becomes 'off limits' for the family, which is totally disruptive to family life. The experience with the police and with other professionals can become the focus of attention for the family for a long time, requiring them to place their grief on hold for a considerable amount of time. The press and media interest in the details of the suicide or murder may be quite intrusive and too intense for the family to cope with, which would not necessarily be the case for many other deaths. The sources of referrals may reflect the different nature of this type of death, coming from doctors in local practices, from community mental health workers, the coroner's court and the police.

One organization that runs these groups usually holds them on a set day of the week on a monthly basis so that it becomes a definite pattern for those who wish to attend. Many of these groups run for two hours with a little more informality than some groups, so that refreshments are on hand throughout and participants help themselves. It is felt that the more informal the setting can be, the better it is for these people, as they encounter a great deal of legality, formality and red tape in what they are experiencing or have gone through.

Those who facilitate groups for people bereaved through murder keep an eye on what is going on in the media. There may be reports on their own clients' specific cases as well as other cases and news items concerning procedures or reforms. These can have ramifications for the participants. So it may be that the facilitators will introduce a topic in the news if it is relevant and see if that initiates a conversation the group wishes to have at that session. Because the bereaved families are often victims themselves of the legal system, there are different needs for these group participants that set them apart from being involved in groups where the death was more natural. But it may also be that, because of this, the numbers are fewer than in other groups, so the facilitators would be advised to be flexible and work with whoever turns up.

I have been particularly interested in a group that has been running in Wellington, New Zealand, called 'Waves', as written up in an article in the journal *Bereavement Care* (Bowden 2011). It is described as a 'psycho-educational programme for adults bereaved by suicide' and is run in a co-facilitated, closed group format over eight weeks by Chris Bowden. It is a programme developed for adults over 17 years of age, regardless of gender and relationship to the deceased. It has been running twice a year since 2006 and accommodates people who have been bereaved at least six months after the death. Those who have been bereaved for a shorter time than six months are placed on a waiting list and also offered interim individual support. Bowden writes:

> *It aims to help the bereaved find meaning in the death; deal with feelings of guilt, blame and personal responsibility; manage feelings of rejection, abandonment, stigmatization and social isolation; and resolve difficulties in family interaction and communication. (Bowden 2011, p.26)*

The sessions last for two hours, with the first hour being 'focused on sharing information, discussing themes and issues, and developing coping skills' (Bowden 2011, p.28). The second hour is allocated to sharing and exploring the participants' own personal grief.

The sessions are made up of the following topics: introductions; understanding the grieving process; the effects of grief and suicide; living with 'why?'; managing the hard times; helping others through the hard times; healing and new beginnings; looking ahead; and closure, feedback and evaluation (Bowden 2011, p.27). The groups are facilitated by Bowden, who is a lecturer at Victoria University of Wellington, and a qualified counsellor (Caroline Cole); they share the sessions, with Chris Bowden leading the first hour and Caroline Cole the second.

> They work together to facilitate learning in small break-out groups (sometimes based on gender, age or circumstances), rotating around the groups as members share strategies, discuss issues and develop their understanding. (Bowden 2011, p.30)

Walking groups

Walking groups have been found to be supportive for people with mental health issues as well as bereavement. One hospice in the East of England has set up a walking group to offer some of the participants a follow-on activity from the open group that is run.

The walking group is called 'Wayfinders', a word play on 'finding your way' through grief. It has been advertised initially through the hospice's support groups but also through the local branch of another bereavement organization and in the cafes at the country park where it is held (see Figure 3.3). It extends to people beyond the hospice's usual criterion, which limits support to those whose relatives died under the care of the hospice.

The aim was to have an activity that would bridge the support groups to others in the community and to assist the group participants in starting to connect socially at a wider level by getting out in an environment where they would feel safe. The organizers have recognized that there can be a huge gulf caused through emotional vulnerability and detachment in their clients' bereavements. Jane Pope, the Bereavement Service Co-ordinator, reports, 'The group has been a huge success and for some has been an absolute lifesaver. One client's GP said he thought it was the best idea he'd heard of in a long time!'

The participants meet in the same location at the same time on the first Thursday of the month at 6.30 p.m. during the months from April to September and the first Saturday at 10.00 a.m. during the months from October to March because of the short winter daylight hours. They walk for about 45–60 minutes and then enjoy refreshments in the cafe or outside by the lake, depending on the weather. There is always a shorter and a longer walk available because some are less able, and they vary the routes. The group is now two years old and continues to grow.

A few months ago, a number of participants said they would like to see a show that was on, and so a volunteer took responsibility for organizing a group booking. As a result of the success of this event, they have requested more socializing events. Jane feels strongly that this needs to be organized by them, so she has set up a database and has requested that those who wish to participate give consent for her to share their contact details with a small group of 'Wayfinders' members who are going to organize social events on the group's behalf. New members will be asked at the point of registration if they want to join the social group as well.

There are a few health and safety issues to consider in this venture – it is not as simple as putting on a pair of walking boots. Designing a form so that participants release the organization from any liability for accident, loss or damage, and informing the park or council where the walk is to take part, are two aspects to be considered.

WAYFINDERS

A Walking Group for Bereaved People

Are you struggling to find your way through grief?
Do you find it more difficult to socialize since your loss?
Wayfinders might be just the thing to help you get back on track.

This is an informal opportunity for people who have been bereaved to socialize with others in an atmosphere of understanding and support.

Come and enjoy the benefits of the great outdoors with specially trained bereavement support volunteers on hand should you need them.

Wayfinders events take place monthly at _____
where the paths are suitable for wheelchair users. After the walk (shorter or longer routes available) stay and have refreshments and a chat.

We meet up at _____

Walkers are responsible for their own safety but are advised to prepare appropriately for the day's weather conditions and carry a mobile phone. You will be asked to provide an emergency contact number before walking.

Please be assured you will be given a warm welcome if you decide to attend **Wayfinders**.

We meet at the _____

October to March (inclusive)
at 10.00 a.m. on the first Saturday of the month.
April to September (inclusive)
at 6.30 p.m. on the first Thursday of the month.

For more details about the walks, please contact:

Figure 3.3 Wayfinders leaflet

Online bereavement support groups

Turning to online computer facilities is becoming a natural way of handling life's challenges for a lot of people. We do our online shopping; we catch up with the news online; we put our symptoms into an online diagnostic system and can get a variety of results before going to the doctor; we can go online to search for a companion or a date; and we can go online to be part of a number of support groups, bereavement included. Millions of users turn on to and use Facebook every month. Social media technology is something that we can ill afford to ignore if we want to support people in our communities by offering them alternative or additional options to meeting in face-to-face groups.

There are websites that already offer bereavement support through groups, but it may be possible to set up your own group linked to your hospice or organization's website. There are several areas to consider, however, when thinking of setting up an online support group:

- the control issue

- the management issue

- the technology issue.

Before you consider setting up a group you would need to think through what it is you want to offer people; what it is you want to achieve; how you can make it a safe place for vulnerable people, which is an ethical issue; and what the cost might be to the organization in monetary terms and in terms of human resources.

With regard to the *control* issue, you would want to consider whether or not you need to make the group a 'closed' group to the membership; that would mean perhaps those particularly from your organization or not. For example, if you are operating from a bereavement service in a hospice, you might want to offer an online group only to those people who are eligible for support in the normal way your hospice offers support, which may not be to the wider community or indeed anyone world-wide. You would also need to consider whether or not you want people only to post their messages on a public board, or wall, or if you would like them to be able to talk to each other privately as well. Privacy is a big consideration for vulnerable people. They would not want their friends and family necessarily to see what they are posting and what they are experiencing on a daily basis. You also need to consider whether you want to offer them peer support rather than a group facilitated by a member of the hospice team, which requires online chat facilities, as well as thinking about the ethical issues around confidentiality and protection. The bereaved people I have spoken to actually wanted to have the flexibility of putting up a message at three o'clock in the morning, if they are still awake and having a bad night.

This leads on to the issue of *management* of the group, which in essence is about taking responsibility for the safety of the group and how to manage it on a daily basis. This would require you to think about how to put in place ways of managing someone who became disrespectful, abusive or inappropriate. There are ways of doing that: for example, by 'post moderation', which means you get to view all the postings before they are posted on the board; or by having a reporting system where people inform you and you are able to block that participant, perhaps after giving warnings of the unacceptability of their behaviour. It would be important to create your own simple terms and conditions for group membership which would enable you to take someone out of the group if they are violating any of those conditions.

After you have thought about control, privacy and the management of the group you can consider what *technology* would be suitable for your needs and those of the bereaved people you wish to reach. Facebook has its own groups and, if your organization has a Facebook page, it is probably integrated to Facebook and will be available to all the users of Facebook, which offers you less control. You can purchase a bespoke forum which would be built to all your specifications concerning access, control and management, though this might be an expensive option. Alternatively, there are companies that can provide a package for creating your own social network which can provide the privacy people would need, one-to-one dialogue facilities, as well as the ability to post videos and photographs. There is a monthly charge depending on the package you opt for and could be a reasonable way forward. (An example of one such company, NING, is listed in the Useful Resources section at the end of the book.)

There are online groups such as the one on Facebook called Widowsover50. In this group bereaved widows and widowers sign up to a membership and are able to post messages 'on the wall' so that all members can see them, and also members are able to 'inbox' each other on a one-to-one private basis.

To illustrate this, Lindy is a widow in her early sixties and has used this group for several months. She says, 'In the first few months after my husband died I was like a lost sheep in the middle of a field, feeling totally bereft and looking everywhere for help.' At about seven weeks after the death of her husband, Lindy attended a group at the local hospice, though she did not feel it helped very much. 'The others were in a different place to me; I would be the only one crying in the group every week. I was just too raw and too emotional at the time.' Looking back at it she feels it was probably too early in her grief to use the group well and get anything valuable from it. (This confirms some of the thoughts about not starting people in groups until at least five or six months after the death, as discussed in Chapter 2.) The facilitator of the group understood this and offered her some further support on a one-to-one basis, which she did find helpful. It was during this time of searching around for help that Lindy found the Facebook group. She had read an article in a magazine about a woman whose husband had died of oesophageal cancer, as Lindy's husband had, and this woman had put the name of the group as a source of reference, so Lindy, already on Facebook, became a member.

There are no mediators or facilitators in this group, so the group supports itself, and although there are 63 members at present, there are a smaller number who regularly post messages 'on the wall'. She began quietly putting messages up about herself generally, though she has never shared too much as she is an extremely private person and would not wish to use the group for expressing herself emotionally. She immediately received messages that were welcoming her and starting up conversations with her. The result of posting messages has been the introduction to two other women who live in the same area and who now message each other through the private inbox. They also meet up regularly and have found friendship together, going out for trips to the theatre and meeting for lunch. The support they give each other is truly helpful for Lindy and she feels she has benefited enormously through the contacts in the group.

Lindy understands that, though it is a private membership group, there is a risk that anyone could become a member under false pretences and start talking in a way that is not acceptable. She said that if that happened she would just come out of the group, having first made her feelings known to the person who started the group through an inbox message. As she rightly says, she is an intelligent person who has worked most of her life, and she knows what she would deem acceptable or otherwise. She also says that people are able to make choices for themselves, and even if they are vulnerable they can still protect themselves by limiting the amount of information they provide.

A note of caution: if you are thinking about setting up a site for bereaved people through your organization, ethical consideration should still be given to the safety of this group of vulnerable people and the management of such groups, so that no one is open to receiving damaging messages or being further hurt by the experience.

Creative groups

Some groups meet specifically to be creative, exploring their grief through different means. There are also ways of working creatively in any group. Let's look first at the group that meets specifically to explore their grief in a creative way.

One way of working in a specifically creative group is to organize a day, or part of a day, or several regular meetings where the participants are working towards a creative group goal. They should be aware of the aim and the required involvement before they commit to it. You may have a project, like decorating glass or ceramic tiles for a wall-mounted display, or making individual squares to be sewn together to form a large 'quilt', which becomes a group activity and each one plays their part in the whole process.

Another form of creative group work is doing smaller creative exercises that are worked on by the individual, and after completion each one comes back from the activity to discuss it in the group or in pairs, as is desired. An example of the type of work that can be done in these groups would be collage work, where participants cut and paste words, images and pictures from magazines onto thick paper or card to depict their journey, or their 'state of being', after their loss. You do not need a sink and pots of paints and brushes for this, so it could be done in a fairly large room with small tables for each person to work on, providing scissors, magazines, glue or paste and various assortments of coloured pens. This can be quite absorbing, and the group work happens in the telling and sharing afterwards. J. Earl Rogers (2007) provides many ideas of what can be done in creative groups and outlines in detail how to run an eight-week 'course' for those who wish to work this way. Jane Moss's (2012) *Writing in Bereavement: A Creative Handbook* is full of ideas for using the written word. She also provides an outline for working in groups.

Apart from organizing a specific group where the sharing is done through the creative activity, there are also several ways of working creatively in groups generally. You can introduce creative activities into the group, from something simple, like reading a poem or an excerpt from a book and then discussing it or sharing photographs, to more involved activities like writing about or depicting some aspect of grief or bereavement. You may be able to introduce the poem, excerpt or photographs into any group, closed or open or a drop-in situation, as these activities require no particular effort on behalf of the participants and they may feel able to participate quite freely or not, as they wish. The other, more active participation through writing or drawing would require the participants to sign up to this way of working in the first place, so they understand what is required of them and what is on offer ahead of time. It is good to start in a small way by introducing some basic ideas to a group and then, once you have gained enough experience and confidence, you can arrange a group that is specifically about sharing grief through creative activities.

In summary, the case studies and descriptions of various groups I have given in this chapter are only some of the ways that I and others have developed our thinking around the concept of groups, and the way participants can be accommodated in different ways. When you have a group of people together you will inevitably have some different styles of relating to consider and different aspects of people's personalities to cope with. In the next chapter we look at some of the challenging behaviours that can be brought into a group and some ways in which to handle them without the group disintegrating – which may be a real fear for us as facilitators.

CHAPTER 4

Managing Dynamics
in the Group

'How do you cope with difficult groups?' This is a question that
frequently gets asked when talking about group work. I suppose my
first response is to say I do not think there are difficult groups per
se; only difficult behaviours to handle in a group that can make a
group function less well. Facilitating a group can be an adventure,
fraught with danger and perils for the unsuspecting, unprepared and
unskilled. There are particular reasons why things can go wrong in
group dynamics, and to help us look at these, I have turned to some
of the professional experts in the field for their advice.

Wolfelt (2004) suggests that problems can arise because of any
one of three reasons:

> 1. Lack of facilitator preparation; 2. Discrepancies between participants'
> expectations and facilitators' expectations; 3. Individual participant
> problems. (Wolfelt 2004, p.69)

The first he identifies as being concerned with the administration,
organization and communication of details about the running of the
group, or perhaps with over-controlling facilitation. I would also add
that it could be any ineffective facilitation style that does not take
control when it should or is not firm enough to guide the group
through some turbulent times. The second is about the mismatched
expectations of the participants and what the group facilitators have in
mind, which probably goes back to the lack of preparation or proper
assessment prior to the group starting. The third is to do with an

individual participant's own style of relating and personality that can cause some challenging times in the group. It is this third area that we are going to look at in this chapter.

It can be difficult sometimes to think on your feet and come up with just the right comment or intervention that will defuse a potential conflict, challenge or behaviour pattern. So perhaps it might be helpful to take some time to think through how you might respond to some of these situations, before you read on to see what suggestions are given. The suggestions given are not by any means exhaustive and not the only solution to coping with difficult behaviours, but are simply some of the ways that prove helpful with some people.

Some potentially difficult behaviours
Take time to reflect on these questions:

- What would you do with a person who constantly wants to take over the discussion and be heard louder and longer than others?

- How might the persistent silence of a participant affect the group as a whole and what might you do to help that participant contribute meaningfully?

- How might you help the distressed and tearful person stay with the group and yet prevent the group from going into a decline?

- What might you do to minimize the effect of the person who dramatizes or catastrophizes situations so that their contributions are irritating to the group as a whole?

I find myself in agreement with those who would say it is rarely a good or wise thing to challenge difficult behaviour openly and in an obvious way in front of the rest of the group (Wolfelt 2004). This is one of those times when there is a real difference with bereavement support groups and counselling therapy groups. In a counselling therapy group, relationships between the different participants and the group facilitators (therapists) and their own relating styles would all become the subject for discussion. In fact, the way people behave in the group will often be seen as the way they handle relationships outside the group so that open and gentle confrontation will be one of the means of bringing about a therapeutic outcome. Corey and Corey (1992) write about using a range of responses in their therapeutic groups:

In co-leading groups, we do not consciously think about what theory we are using with what clients... We are inclined to use more confrontive interventions with relatively well-functioning members, for example, and to draw on supportive approaches when we work with clients who are unable to benefit from confrontation. (Corey and Corey 1992, p.7)

Maybe it would be helpful to remind ourselves that each participant deserves to be respected for who they are – a hurting and struggling individual who is trying to come to terms with the tragic loss of a loved one. It is all too easy for facilitators, especially after the group has left and in the debrief that follows, to label somebody as 'difficult', 'dominating', 'resistant' or a 'know-it-all'. By falling into the trap of labelling the participant as their behaviour, we can fail to take on board what they are going through, how they are affected and what happens for them when they come to a bereavement group. In a bereavement support group, facilitators are present to assist the participants on their journey of grief and adaptation to their new life; a life characterized sometimes by pain and sorrow but, we hope, eventually, by some measure of personal development. The personal development that is at the core of a counselling therapy group, however, is probably not what a bereaved person is looking for from a support group. I would suggest that we adopt what Corey and Corey (1992) refer to as 'supportive approaches' with our participants when handling difficult behaviours. A gentle challenge may have to be done, but away from the group's eyes and ears. Therefore, I would recommend that you try to handle people's particular behaviours outside the group if possible. After all, no one wants to feel as if they are being told off, and no one wants to feel humiliated in front of others. However, there are a few ways of managing some behaviours inside the group, and these are what we will be considering here.

OVERBEARING OR DOMINATING BEHAVIOURS

We have probably all met them in different places in our lives, on courses, at social gatherings, at work and in meetings. They are those people who talk over us and over others and who seem to enjoy the limelight. They can be male or female, young or old, but they all seem to have a similar intent, to make sure you listen to them and hear what they have to say. When they appear in a support group, it can be really difficult to handle their behaviour, but unless it is managed in some measure, the group may disintegrate. People may slowly withdraw, initially by not talking, and then by leaving the group. There are various ways these participants present their behaviours, but one of the most usual ways is identified by Corey and Corey (1992):

> *This member is continually 'identifying with others' – that is, taking others' statements as openings for detailed stories about his or her own life... They may be talking excessively out of anxiety, they may be accustomed to being ignored, or they may be attempting to keep control of the group. (Corey and Corey 1992, p.157)*

Let me illustrate this behaviour with a participant, Wilf, who attended a winter group. Wilf had already shown some anxious and slightly demanding behaviours in the pre-group telephone conversations the facilitator, Jo, had with him. In the first of these conversations, he insisted he did not want individual support as he wanted to talk with people who had gone through similar things to himself and experienced the death of a spouse. Jo spent some time telling him about the way the groups were run and some of the advantages and disadvantages of groups, and that he would be called at the beginning of September to let him know further details. In the middle of August, however, he began making several phone calls leaving messages that Jo was to call him. In her conversation with him she was aware of an energy that she was concerned about, but it was not significant enough for her to consider advising him not to come.

When attending the group in the first session, Wilf presented as a brusque, bluntly spoken man who suffered no fools. He immediately proceeded to take over the conversations in the refreshment area before the group started. Several approaches had to be adopted with Wilf throughout the group sessions, as not one single approach seemed to work successfully, though he did settle into the group process to some degree after around the third or fourth sessions. The approaches used are given below.

Doing the 'round'

The first approach that was necessary to adopt in the first session was to ask the participants for specific input, then go round the group for each one's input. This was after the introductions and ground rules discussion. Jo was quite explicit in her instructions:

> 'It would be helpful perhaps for all of us to know a little about each other and the story of your spouse or partner's illness, if you wish to tell us. We'll do this in a "round", which means we'll go round and allow each one of you about five to ten minutes to talk without interruption, so that you can tell us a little of your story. You won't be able to tell us all of it today because of time constraints. I hope you won't feel offended if I tell you your time is up, as we want to make sure everyone has enough time. We won't be commenting on each story, just listening to each other at the moment. Let's start with…'

Jo started with a participant a little away from Wilf so that he would not be the last to go. It went well for time-keeping and sharing with the first two participants. But when it came to the third participant, Wilf began to interrupt with comments like, 'That's how I am' or 'That's how it was for me.' With these comments he began to tell his story. Jo had to interrupt him to remind him they were doing this 'round' without interruptions:

> 'Excuse me, Wilf, just a reminder that we're allowing Paul to tell his story first, without commenting. We'll come to your story afterwards and you'll get your time.'

When they got to Wilf, he was a little caustic in his comment, 'Oh, is it my turn now?' Jo nodded, 'Yes, you have five to ten minutes and then I'll have to stop you if you go over.'

It did not feel an easy place for any of them, as it felt that Wilf was already vying to dominate and make himself felt. Jo did indeed have to intervene to tell him his time was up. It does not feel easy to talk over someone and stop them in mid-flow, but this is one of the ways we are able to establish the rules and stick to them for the benefit of the whole group.

> 'I'm sorry, I'll have to stop you there, Wilf. Thanks for sharing – that's your time up for this round, but there will be further opportunities to finish the details of your story at another time. For this session, it's really important that everyone gets a chance to share, so that no one is left out. I'm sure you'll agree with me on that.'

Jo could see he did not like it, but everyone in the group did manage to tell something of their story in the first session. It was important for them all to speak, if they wished to, so that they were not deprived of their opportunity to share in the first session.

Using humour

After a few sessions, Wilf was still quite dominating, but not trying to take over as frequently as in the first two sessions. There were one or two others who were quite talkative too, so if Jo said anything in general about this, she knew it would also fit others and not spotlight Wilf in particular. Jo knew by now that Wilf had a dry sense of humour, but she needed to make it clear when she was using humour to handle a situation. So she started the next group session by asking one of the quieter members to begin with her check-in. Jo said:

> 'Perhaps we can begin today with Daphne, who hasn't been able to get much of a word in up till now with all of you chatty ones.'

There was a little bit of laughter, and one of the 'chatty' ones, Jackie, said, 'You're right, we are a chatty bunch, aren't we? We should let others have more of a go.' She looked at Wilf and another woman with a nod of the head and a knowing wink. The session went remarkably well after that; they had obviously taken Jackie's comment on board.

Using a hand gesture

On one occasion, Jo had to adopt a more directive tactic. She had to stop Wilf in mid-flow, using a hand gesture like a traffic warden stopping the oncoming traffic:

> 'Wilf, we're listening to Mary now, we'll come back to your comments afterwards. But we need to allow Mary to finish.' And to Mary, 'Go on Mary, you were saying...'

One sentence

Another time, Jo had to stop Wilf in mid-flow because there was such a jumble of words that it was not making a lot of sense, as if he was trying to get it all out quickly before he was stopped. So Jo interrupted him:

> 'Wilf, I'm sorry to do this, but you're talking so fast and with so many details that I for one am struggling to understand and I've got a bit lost. Can you sum up in one sentence or one word what you want to say?'

He was not able to keep to one word, of course, or even one sentence, but he did focus his thoughts and finish quite quickly after that.

Select an extract

They had listened to Wilf's story about his sons and the painful relationship he had with one in particular, and after giving him the air-space, Jo selected a pertinent part out of what he had told them and then asked others to comment on what they had heard.

> 'Wilf, you've shared some hard things about your relationship with your sons, but I've heard you say that you wouldn't have wanted it this way. I wonder if we could ask other people to say what they've heard in your story and give you some feedback. Perhaps you can listen to each one.'

This was a bit risky to do as Jo thought Wilf would want to comment on all their observations, and hog the floor again, but in fact it seemed to please him that they were focusing on him for a while. Immediately after they had finished (and not everyone did make comments) Jo asked him to give one sentence back as a response, and he said, 'I just want to thank you for listening and understanding.' After that he did become a little less dominating, and he did give the other participants enough space to speak, though he was not always able to resist butting in.

Perhaps because of the strategies taken in the early group sessions, Wilf's behaviour was not sufficiently distracting and disruptive to have to take the option below.

Speak to them outside the group

If all else fails, you should probably talk to them outside the group. This was done in one instance where the group facilitator had to speak to a woman who was so desperate to talk and to contribute that it had become quite irritating to the group and a few participants had started giving each other looks across the space as if to say, 'Here she goes again!'

After a group session where this had happened, Pauline, the group facilitator, asked Beryl if she could spare a few moments to talk or if she, Pauline, could come to visit before the next session, which was in another two weeks' time. Pauline had made sure she had caught Beryl after the others had left the group session, and Beryl was fine to have a few quiet words after the group. (Pauline and her co-facilitator, Gerry, had agreed previously at their debriefing session that they would need to address this with Beryl if the behaviour had persisted in that session.) The conversation went something like this:

Pauline: How are you finding the group sessions, Beryl? Are they beneficial for you?

Beryl: Oh, yes, they are. They're a lifeline for me. I wouldn't miss them for anything. I can't wait until the next one – I would come every week if you had a group meeting. I just think I'm getting so much out of it.

Pauline: That sounds really encouraging; it's your enthusiasm about the group that's special. What are you getting in particular from the sessions, do you think?

Beryl: Well, it's just lovely to listen to others talk and hear what they're going through, because it's so much like what I'm experiencing – it's so good isn't it that we all feel so much the same?

Pauline: It's good you feel that way, Beryl, because one of the biggest benefits is that people can share and identify with others and...

At this point, Beryl interrupts.

Beryl: Oh yes. It's so good for me to know that I'm not going mad; I do feel sometimes that I am going mad, you know. It can be quite lonely when you're on your own and don't have anyone to share with during the day, like I used to share with Frank.

Her eyes fill with tears and she starts to dab her eyes with a tissue.

Pauline: It can be lonely, that's why the group is so important to you and to everyone. But I want to mention something that in fact has just happened between us. I was just talking and you interrupted me and...

Beryl: I'm so sorry, Pauline. I didn't do it on purpose.

Pauline: (*Smiling*) I think it just happened again.

Beryl: Oh.

Pauline: I think what I see in the group is that you are so eager to share and so glad to be here with the others that you want to join in with everything that is said. This means though that some of the people don't really get to finish what they're saying before you interrupt them. I heard it today, for example, when Chris was talking about her husband's ashes and what to do with them, and you came in with what you've decided to do. I wonder what you think Chris might have felt like when she hadn't been able to finish talking about this concern she has and I had to bring her back in later.

Beryl: (*Getting a bit defensive and starting to tear up*) I don't know what she might have felt like... Maybe I shouldn't be here; maybe if everyone thinks I'm a nuisance I should stay away!

Pauline: I can see that you're feeling a bit emotional about this but I'm not at all suggesting that you stay away. You're just as important to the group as the others are, and you have just said how much you're getting from it and...

Beryl: Yes, but if they're all thinking bad of me, I don't want to come.

Pauline: That would be very sad for you and the rest of us and not what I was asking you to think about. Beryl, it happened again and you didn't notice that you'd interrupted me, did you?

Beryl: No, I didn't.

Pauline: Well, what I'm asking you to think about is letting people carry on until they've finished speaking and then, if you have anything to say, maybe you can look to see if anyone else wants to say something before you go ahead. (*Very gently*) All I'm really suggesting is that you might do a little more listening to the others, as you said you really think this is one of the most valuable things you get from the group.

Beryl: Yes, it is, but I don't want them to think I'm an awful person – I thought they all liked me and now I don't know if they do.

Pauline: You're perhaps feeling a bit insecure now as you're so

positive about the group and really enthusiastic about it and I've
pointed out something that has upset you. But I don't think there really
is any sign that anyone thinks you're an awful person. I've seen you
chatting together with Mike and Chris and others on many occasions
and you've gone out for coffee, you've told me, with Chris. So I really
don't think that anyone is thinking badly about you. What this is about
is just helping you to try to rein in your enthusiasm and let others have
more time to speak.

Beryl: Oh well, I'll have to see. I'm not sure. I'll have to go now anyway.

Pauline: I can see that this has really impacted you, but I do want you
to know that we still want you to keep coming to the group, as you
have so much that is valuable to give. I wonder if in the week you
might like to contact me, or possibly Gerry, and perhaps have a chat
with him, as I'm sure he'd be glad to do that with you.

That ended the conversation, and Pauline felt unsure as to whether
Beryl would come again. With a heavy heart, Pauline debriefed with
Gerry, so that he knew what had transpired. Later in the week, Gerry
did get a call from Beryl asking if she could come and talk to him
before the next group. Informing Pauline this had happened, Gerry
met with Beryl. At this meeting Beryl wanted to say how she had felt
when Pauline had spoken to her and to find out if Gerry agreed with
Pauline. He gently listened and heard her out, and then explained that
he had noticed the same thing that Pauline had and gave her one or
two examples. Beryl remembered the examples because they had been
when others had been quite emotional and Beryl had interrupted, out
of a desire to help them or 'rescue' them in their pain. Gerry was able
to explore this with Beryl and help her see how people needed to have
the freedom to express their pain in the group and that she did not
have to help them out. He explored with her how she felt when this
happened to others and how it brought up her own pain. This session
proved to be a turning point for Beryl, and she went on to attend the
group, remaining quieter but still making her contributions, so that
she was able to hear and listen to others and gain from the experience,
while the other participants genuinely responded to her in a positive
way and affirmed her.

It is always a risk speaking to someone about their behaviour,
because they are often not aware of the impact they are having on

others, and you have to go gently with them, giving positive feedback, and then gently pointing out what you have observed that might have an impact on the others in the group. It would be helpful to have some examples so that you can take them back to a specific incident to think about, if they are willing to do so. It might also be helpful to offer them another opportunity to talk about it again when they have had time to think about it or, as Pauline did, offer the services of the co-facilitator who also has made observations of the behaviour.

Sadly, you may have to be prepared for the person to remove themselves completely from the group as they are free to make the decision for themselves. It is most unfortunate if this happens, and perhaps you can contact them to offer individual support, though realistically few people would be prepared to take it up. The impact on us as facilitators can be quite considerable when this happens. Because of the nature of the people we are, there can be a real sense of guilt, failure or insecurity about our actions and words after someone rejects the service we are providing. This is one of those situations when good supervision is beneficial, before the participant is spoken to, if at all possible. It is certainly most useful after the event, so as to deal with your own feelings and also to check out how you actually handled the situation. The more honest you can be about this, the more you will learn from the experience and develop your skills.

SILENT BEHAVIOURS

Silences often happen in a group. Some silences are planned, like asking participants to take a minute or two to think about, or meditate on, something; some silences happen spontaneously at the end of a discussion when participants are thinking about what has been said, or there comes a need for the next subject to be raised. This is a kind of natural conversational silence. There are also participants who are by nature quiet and possibly reserved. These participants are not resistant to sharing – they just do not find it very easy to do it in a group. They are happy to be part of a group and to be active listeners.

To illustrate this, Dennis, who was the facilitator in the closed group case study in Chapter 3, tells of a participant who was very quiet in a group he ran, although she would occasionally come out with a few things if she was asked. At the end of the group in the final session, Dennis asked the participants what they had got out of coming to the group, and her response surprised him:

> 'I know I haven't talked a lot, and I want to thank you for not forcing me to, but I have gained so much from being here and listening to all that you've had to say. I've benefited from being part of the group and I now know I'm not on my own. When I start to get lonely or depressed, I shall think of what we've talked about here and I shall know I've got friends who feel the same.'

Of all the participants, Dennis had been most concerned for her, as she had not shared a lot in the sessions. For him this was a salutary lesson about those who are quiet. As a result of this lesson, he will often say in the introductory session about the ground rules that it is fine not to say very much if people do not want to, until they feel ready to participate.

It is not the quiet ones who say very little but are active by their very presence that I want to discuss here. Rather, I want to discuss the silent behaviour that becomes noticeable and perhaps uncomfortable for the group. This has something to do with the participant's energy and motivation for the silent behaviour.

The question was posed at the beginning of the chapter about how the persistent silence of a participant might affect the group as a whole, and the question implicitly assumes that there might be some impact. It does appear to be the case, from my observations, that saying and doing nothing in a group can have as much impact as what is actually said and done. Someone who says almost nothing in a group may be supported at the beginning by the others if they feel that the person is too upset or too shy initially to say anything. If that silence continues into the second or third sessions, however, the other participants may start to feel uncomfortable and less sympathetic, if they feel that there is more to it than shyness or feeling upset. When participants are expressing difficult emotions or sharing some of the closest things about their loved ones, their situation or their family, they may get suspicious of another in the group who continues to be silent. They may begin, rightly or wrongly, to feel judged or criticized in some way by this person. The rest of the group may begin to wonder if the silent participant is resisting making an effort, or trying to control them in some strange way. There may be varying reasons for someone's silence and so it might be helpful to refer to some expert advice.

Corey and Corey (1992) make some helpful suggestions about this type of behaviour which indicate that there are often more acceptable reasons than the suggested dubious ones others might attribute to the silent participant.

> *There are many reasons for nonparticipating behavior; and these should be explored. Some of the reasons are:*
>
> - *the feeling that one doesn't have anything worthwhile to say*
>
> - *the feeling that one shouldn't talk about oneself or that one should be seen and not heard*
>
> - *the fear of looking foolish; not knowing the appropriate thing to say or do*
>
> - *the fear of certain members in the group or of the authority of the group leader*
>
> - *resistance, particularly if the person doesn't really want to be a member of the group*
>
> - *uncertainty about how the group process works*
>
> - *fear of being rejected or of being accepted*
>
> - *lack of trust in the group; fear of leaks of confidentiality.*
>
> *(Corey and Corey 1992, p.156)*

The first three suggestions above, as well as the fear of being rejected or of being accepted, seem to emanate from insecurity in the participant. They do not feel secure in themselves to share in a group; they feel others have something better to offer and they will only appear foolish as they struggle to get their thoughts out in a coherent sentence; and they fear rejection or acceptance. It may be that this participant is not used to having their opinions listened to or being respected, or that they are afraid of opening up because the experience of being vulnerable feels too big, along with the grief they already feel.

One way to handle this might be to help them make small attempts to say something in the group by asking specific questions for the entire group to answer. Not – 'What has been the biggest struggle for you this week?' This might be an appropriate question for a fully functioning group, but not in this instance where a participant is not participating. It might be helpful rather to ask something like:

> 'What job (task, project) did you manage to do this week?'

Or:

> 'What company (visitor) or little happening have you had this week that was pleasant?'

This can be something small that is positive for the participants to focus on, in order to bring out their confidence, where they can be brief and specific or give a bit more detail if they choose to do so. It might be helpful if you employed a 'round' in order to get the group going and offer the participant an opportunity to join in. You might be mindful of not always starting with the quiet participant in order to make sure they start, but rather to include them in the early contributions so that they do not have too much time to get nervous, but have enough time to think about something to say.

The fear of the authority figure may come from a lack of experience with people generally and may inhibit them in taking any risks at all, so letting someone settle in for a time in order to feel more comfortable with the situation and the facilitators' roles is only reasonable. If despite all the encouragement to talk the participant is still not volunteering, it may be helpful for the rest of the group to understand what is going on for the participant. So it may be possible to say something like:

> 'Pete, we've been meeting for a couple of sessions now and we still don't know very much about what's going on for you. I wonder if perhaps you might be able to tell us a little bit about what you're doing with yourself, or how the group is helping you?'

You might well get something really positive back about how it helps to sit and listen to others, or how the participant feels too overwhelmed to talk very much. Perhaps he feels the companionship is worthwhile. Whatever it is, his comments may satisfy the others in the group that he is not sitting there in judgement on them, or resisting the group. You might make the decision to have that conversation outside the group, when he can speak about his real feelings on a one-to-one basis. It may be that someone in the group is the problem for him, and this is more likely to be aired outside the group than inside.

If someone is in the group but not really wishing to be there, again this should be addressed outside the group and brought out in private. Someone who resists because they do not wish to be there will most probably appear quite defensive or even hostile. It is unusual for someone who does not like the group experience to prolong their attendance at the group sessions, but if it becomes apparent that they appear uncomfortable, it would be good to follow it up outside the group and perhaps offer some individual support. In speaking to the participant outside the group you can refer back to what was said at the initial contracting session:

> 'Pete, at the first session, we talked about the fact that groups aren't for everyone or are not everyone's thing. You seemed a bit uncomfortable in the session so I wondered if that's true for you.'

A participant may be silent because they are uncertain about how the group process works. At the initial session, most participants can experience some sort of anxiety or apprehension and, although you might have acknowledged this and addressed it in your introduction, their anxiety level may be so high that they have not fully taken on board the expectations about contributing to the group process. Again, gentle encouragement to share small things might be enough for them to settle in and find their voice. If they continue in not contributing, you may have to use one of the above tactics and address it outside the group.

Another issue may well be derived from someone's sense of privacy being violated or personal barriers being affronted. Some people do not naturally share, so the level of personal disclosure in the group may be a threat to them in the sense of being too big to cope with, or a fear that they are expected to share at the same level. It may be they experience a lack of trust in the group, rightly or wrongly. If, in their eyes, the level of disclosure is inappropriate, their silence may be a way of showing their disapproval, which will be felt by others in the group. A lack of willingness to share may also come from the fear of leaks in confidentiality. Addressing the confidentiality issue again may bring out some of the issues. For some people, trust can be a long time in the making, so time might or might not assist them to share comfortably. If people are genuinely concerned about the lack of confidentiality then this should be addressed with some specifics, first outside the group and then, if necessary, inside.

There may also be an occasion when a participant has felt pressure, again rightly or wrongly, from the group concerning some thinking or behaviour that has been challenged. This can result in the participant clamming up and not offering too much of themselves in the group for fear of being 'attacked'. They might also become resentful of the facilitators' perceived lack of support in this situation.

An illustration of this would be Wendy, who attended a closed group and had talked quite openly in the first five sessions, but seemed to have become withdrawn after that. The facilitators recognized this and, in supervision after the sixth session, they talked about it. The supervisor asked what it was that had been discussed during the fifth session that Wendy had participated in. They quickly realized the group had been talking about the ashes of their loved ones and what was happening to them. Wendy had her husband's ashes at home but was seriously thinking about putting them in the garden where she could feel her husband's presence. He had apparently taken a great interest in the garden. One of the other participants asked what her husband's family thought about this as it might mean that they wouldn't be able to visit when they wanted to. The point was also made that a public crematorium or cemetery was available most times and days to all the public without having to request 'visiting rights' or get keys to the back gate or front door. Because this participant was a woman in her early forties, there was also this suggestion:

> 'If you were to get into another relationship at any time, it might not be so easy for his family to come and visit, as they might not want to disturb you. They may even feel put out that you're in another relationship.'

The facilitators had not picked up that Wendy had taken any offence at the time, and certainly the group had been quite gentle in their discussion around this subject. But it seemed that Wendy's silence stemmed from that session. The group had two further sessions to run, and the facilitators decided that it was probably better to allow the group to move on rather than address the issue at this point. Wendy did not appear to be allowing it to affect her relationships with the other participants, but her silence was noticeable.

If the group had a longer life to run, or if this had happened in an open group, it might have been helpful to address the issue at the start of another session, with something like:

> 'We've been able to talk quite freely about a number of things in our sessions and I wonder if we can just look at what it's like to have disagreements within the group and how that might feel. There may be times when someone encounters what to them might feel like disapproval from others who don't hold the same beliefs or opinions. What does it feel like to be on the other end of disagreement, I wonder?'

At this point, they could talk in general about it or they could address the particular issue that Wendy appeared to be struggling with.

As a final comment about the silent participant, I would like to suggest that there could be a case for reviewing the ground rules halfway through the allotted sessions, for the closed groups, or at an appropriate time for open groups. The group can be asked how they think they are doing with the ground rules, addressing each point and asking for comments. If the group is being honest they should be able to admit if something makes them uncomfortable. If the ground rules spoke of staying quiet in the first place, the subject could be revisited by asking if they are still OK with this rule, and if they wish to add anything to it.

TEARFUL, DISTRESSED AND EMOTIONAL BEHAVIOURS

It would be a normal thing in a bereavement support group to experience tears and sometimes gentle sobbing when someone has connected with a painful feeling or memory. This is part of the ebb and flow of supporting hurting people. However, what is ordinary for some will be uncomfortable for others. The question given near the beginning of the chapter was: how might you help the distressed and tearful person stay with the group and yet prevent the group from going into a decline?

First, have a look at what you are comfortable with. Ask yourself, 'What are my comfort levels in terms of tears and sobbing?' Bear in mind this might be different in an individual session from what it is in a group setting. I have found that I can be quite empathic without always being touched by someone's pain. I show that empathy in the words I use to communicate my understanding and my compassion. There are other times when someone's tears touch me and I feel the tears in my own eyes, something has been transmitted from the client to me, or their words or feelings have evoked something of my own experience. There are other times when I am not drawn to the tears of the person in front of me and I can usually safely assume, because I know I am quite compassionate and soft-hearted, that there is something about the tears that I do not trust, or maybe they are false tears, or tears for effect. You may come across all these during the process of a support group and possibly even within one session.

So recognizing what is going on in the group and in yourself might be important when someone starts to cry. There will be all sorts of reactions in the group: some will want to fix the situation; someone will want to put an arm around the person; someone might start a different subject in embarrassment; and some may not be aware that anything is happening at all. What the facilitator can do is intervene so that the person is not ignored and the group can rest with the situation. It might be enough to say to the group:

> 'We need to just stay with Mary for a while so she feels we are here for her, and can experience our support. Mary, we can't fix the pain for you, so we're going to let you feel those tears – take your time and then we'll come back to you.'

Silence may follow for a short time, and then you might ask her if she is able to talk about what was going on for her. If she is still unable to talk, you can offer an alternative.

> 'It's difficult for you to talk right now, Mary, and we appreciate that it might be uncomfortable with the attention focused on you. So if it's OK with you, I'm going to ask the group how they're feeling and what's going on for them. Would anyone like to tell me what they're experiencing right now as they see Mary's sadness?'

At this point someone in the group may be able to share what Mary's tears mean for them, how they have been touched and what they are doing with the feelings. If there is no one who volunteers, you can talk about your own responses or your co-facilitator can offer their contribution, which may be enough to encourage others to share. When, and if, Mary is able to speak, you can go back to her to see how she feels and what she might want from the group by way of support now.

You might also want to address the change in mood of the group session:

> 'We have experienced a lot of emotions and I feel the mood of the group has changed, which is the way it happens for you in your grief journey. You may feel fine one minute and then feel ravaged by emotions and tears the next, with little understanding of why or how it has happened. What do you do to move on from those "flash floods" of pain or sadness?'

By acknowledging what has happened and having stayed with it, you can now move on to enable the group to think about how they deal with those situations at home or when they are out of the house or in company.

We obviously expect to see tears and sobs and a level of distress in a bereavement support group. But there are behaviours that can be difficult for groups to support. For instance, there is the participant who cries excessively so that it feels like 'over-the-top tears' or 'unreal tears'.

As an illustration, Dan was facilitating a particular group and, during the first session, one participant, Gwen, was not able to speak at all, even to say her name or give any details about her husband, who had died. She hung her head with her long dark hair covering her face, and wiped away tears with tissues. In his gentle way, Dan introduced Gwen, saying he understood she was not able to do it as she was too upset. She was still too upset at the end of the session, and Dan expressed at the check-out that he hoped she would feel able to come back to the group the following week. She nodded and he took this as assent. At the following session, she did in fact speak, but as she did so she was wailing. She had silently wept at the first session but now this was really loud and upsetting for the others in the group. Through her tears she was talking in gulps, making it difficult to hear her. Dan was patient with her, but he could see that others were getting uncomfortable. In fact the tears felt strange and not very real. He said to her, as she paused for breath:

> 'Gwen, can I just say something here? I can see that you're very upset as you talk about your husband. But the way you're telling the story to us is making it difficult to understand what you're saying. I wonder

if you could pause here a second or two and if possible start again in a quieter way so that we can hear you. If it's better for you that we come back to you in a few minutes, then we'll do that. What would you like to do?'

Dan had given her a choice and she had to make a decision. A rational decision was expected of her, so she said she would try to continue. She did, though it was still a little affected by her gulps. Dan was kind in his feedback and affirmed her for being able to share her story.

'Thank you, Gwen. You've been able to share some of your story which is progress from last week, and I'm sure we'll hear more as we go on. I hope in the future sessions that you'll be able to talk without getting too upset. Having done it once, it probably won't be as difficult for you again.'

Gently but firmly Dan was giving her the message and expectation that she would be able to share without getting too out of control. Gwen's behaviour felt a little too dramatic, and the facilitators began to expect something from her at each group session, and so did the rest of the group. The participants were not overly sympathetic towards her but they tolerated her. She appeared to want hers to be the worst story, to be the saddest person in the group; she appeared to want everyone's sympathy, and sadly because of her behaviour she did not get what she wanted. There felt like there was a 'pull' for everyone to feel sorry for her and to treat her carefully, as a special case.

The person who dramatizes or catastrophizes situations may be wanting the attention from the group, as Gwen might have, but their contributions can become irritating to the group as a whole. It is important to be careful about confronting these behaviours too directly as the participant may create a bigger scene in the group. Gwen at times seemed to want to be the 'special case' that everyone was thinking about and focusing on. You might be able to use this by saying something like:

'Gwen, you know sometimes it can feel helpful, I'm sure, to have everyone's input. But I'm just wondering if it is sometimes less helpful for you, as if the whole issue just got a lot bigger than it really is. Sometimes we can get things out of proportion by worrying about them like a dog with a bone. Perhaps some of the others have experience of that, too?' (Opening it out to the group.)

It may be necessary, however, to speak to the participant outside the group before somebody in the group gets really irritated and says something damaging to the participant in particular and to the group as a whole. Asking them if you can come to see them at home or see them in the office might be pleasing to them, as they are getting more attention. However, it would also be good to be mindful that sometimes people who adopt these behaviours might also become aggressive or defensive when confronted. It might be advisable for both facilitators to be present, to have a witness to what is being said and how it is said. You might want to address it by saying that you really appreciate that there are some big things that she is facing, but adding that sometimes it feels as if she is making things bigger than they are, and then asking her what that is about for her.

Corey and Corey (1992) reflect on this type of behaviour with regard to the participant who is always emotional, so that everything is a big deal, other people's situations make them cry or they talk about feeling someone's pain for them in a way that feels less than genuine. The person who does this always ensures that the attention is on them, away from the other person who has expressed the pain or sadness in the first place. In their example, it is Lori who is being emotionally reactive:

> *Perhaps she believes that the only way to be productive in the group is to be highly cathartic and, consequently, to be seen by the leader as a 'good' member. She can be deceiving herself in thinking that she is 'really working' when she cries so easily and frequently. This behavior can also serve as a defense because others are likely to hesitate in confronting her. In Lori's case it is not so much a matter of her being sad. Instead, her issues are wanting attention from people – wanting to be liked, accepted and approved of. Her fear may be that if she does not display emotions most of the time, she will be ignored. In some ways, she may be clinging to her problems so that she can keep being emotionally reactive. Her emotionalism is an indirect way of getting what she wants. (Corey and Corey 1992, p.168)*

Corey and Corey (1992) suggest that it is important to be able to determine between what might be a genuine struggle for this person and an appropriate response, and what might be a useful but counterproductive strategy.

INAPPROPRIATE DISCLOSURES

In a group of people who start to share things about their lives, it might be expected that some details of life are going to be shared that are quite poignant and sometimes painful, hurtful and difficult to recall. There may be an opportunity for a participant to explore a difficult marriage with the group, and one of the reasons they are in the group is because the relationship was ambivalent and they need support in finding a way through it. It may be that the participant does not realize that they will share things about themselves that are deeply troubling. I think we can probably allow for that to happen and be grateful sometimes that it does, because it can be quite cathartic for the participants to experience.

However, there are some things that a group may not be prepared for and may not be able to accommodate because they have come with a simple expectation of being supported in a group of people who are experiencing similar feelings and changes in their life. They are not expecting to hear about psychological problems from the past that might have affected another participant. I am not sure if it is ever possible to screen for every eventuality or everyone's past experiences. You may describe ahead of time what the group is for and what its aims are, but you may still get people who give the group too much information or information that is too intimate in detail. Where the information is made known to you prior to the group, it would be wise to explore with the person as to whether they would be able to keep that information to themselves or indeed if they felt another type of group therapy would be more appropriate for them rather than this group focusing on bereavement. While the bereavement may be the most recent issue and they want to have support for that, some people's hinterland issues come to the fore and demand attention.

Establishing what to do with this in the ground rules might be one way of handling situations like this ahead of time. So in addition to the other questions we looked at in discussing ground rules in Chapter 3, you may wish to add another one along the lines of:

> 'What do you think should be acceptable to discuss at our meetings? Sometimes people have experienced really difficult things. How would you want to handle something that was disclosed that was difficult in nature?'

Even when you have discussed it in the ground rules, there may still be times when someone starts revealing details that are too deep or disturbing for the group. You need to be alert to the way the disclosure is being made and perhaps head it off at the pass. For example:

> 'Harry, I'm going to stop you there, because I think you're going to be talking about something that might not be appropriate to bring up in this particular group setting. I wonder if you and I can make time outside the group to talk about it. I hope that will be OK by the rest of you. Sometimes there are things that have happened in our past that need to be addressed, but they require special attention, and perhaps this isn't the place for that kind of work.'

If the participant is agreeable to this, you will still need to deal with the change in atmosphere of the group. Something like this might be honest and suitable:

> 'We might need to rethink where we are now, as what Harry has said has probably had some impact already on other people. I know it has on me. I for one have experienced a bit of shock, as I didn't know about this before. I'm not sure if as a group you want to comment on this or what you would like to do. Perhaps we could address this now?'

If something has been alluded to rather than talked about in detail, it might be easier to make a suggestion that it would be better to leave it alone. But if the disclosure has gone too far, it will need to be addressed. Some groups may just try to ignore it, move around it and move on. Some groups could be paralysed by the disclosure and not be able to move on. However they respond, they will have been impacted by the story, and the situation will need careful handling by the facilitator.

The reason for making some inappropriate disclosure may be quite complex and varied: perhaps the participant feels comfortable with the group and wants to entrust them with something big; or perhaps they are testing out the group's approval of them; or maybe there is an element of wanting to shock, or disrupt. There may even be a feeling of 'You in your nice little worlds won't understand what it's like in my world and I'll give you something to shock you all.' There is an element of disrespect about this behaviour. Whatever the reason might be, the participant needs to be seen outside the group and offered alternative support if that is what is wanted. Unfortunately their place in the group might already have been jeopardized by their disclosure, so the support at this time will be in helping them either to find something more suitable, or to reintegrate into the group, if at all possible.

CONFLICT BETWEEN THE PARTICIPANTS

I have already referred above to something that might bring about some antagonism or conflict in a group, where one of the participants may feel that they are different from the others because of life experiences or of perceived 'class' differences. Where there are obvious differences such as race or sexual orientation, groups may appear to be quite accommodating of the differences and accepting of the individual. The class divide feels more subtle and subjective. It may be that the one who feels most different is fighting their own inner battle rather than the group's disapproval. It would be extremely strange, though, for a number of people to come together over a period of time and for there never to be any form of conflict. Conflict may promote a healthy approach to life as we readjust our comfort zones and expand our ways of thinking. Conflict is not always welcomed though. A lot of us normally wish to take avoidance tactics, and try to smooth over the cracks so that we can get on again. In a group, conflict can become destructive, as it may threaten the group's function as a safe place to be.

Where there is conflict between life experiences, maybe it is possible to explore these differences so that each party can gain. Rather than take the part of the referee, the facilitator has to be more like a mediator. So when differences occur, it is about pointing them out and seeing what can come out of it. For example:

> 'I'm sensing that there is a bit of a struggle going on between Pete and Andy, with some differences of opinions over the way to handle the family in the matter of the possessions and property. Perhaps the differences are because you come from different family backgrounds with different ways of doing things. How would it be if, Pete, you told us a little bit about the way your family has coped with difficult issues in the past, and then perhaps Andy could give us a picture of his family and we might see where the differences lie?'

It is important not to take sides and important not to try to rescue anyone. Where there are misunderstandings, in my experience, it has seldom proved helpful to try to explain what someone else is trying to say, as if they had failed in their communication skills. It would be more helpful to suggest that there might be a misunderstanding and to ask if there would be another way for them to explain what they mean.

When I have come up against a very dogmatic approach to something, I have usually intervened with something like:

> 'Pete, that's certainly one way of looking at it and I suspect you feel quite strongly about it. I wonder if there are any other ways of looking at it that others have which they'd like to express.'

Differences can be welcomed, antagonism can be diffused and the group can accommodate a variety of behaviours as long as the facilitation is appropriate and honest.

RELATIONSHIPS THAT EMERGE

We would probably be happy for our groups to exist in harmony and camaraderie where everyone liked everyone else and got on with each other really well. That is the ideal for support groups and it sometimes happens. However, what can happen is that two or three get on in a group and meet up outside and start to form a clique. They let it be known that they make contact outside the group, and when there are refreshment breaks they are all together, to the exclusion of others. It can be good for participants to have these connections outside the group as they offer each other support and encouragement. What can be more difficult is when there are obvious divides in the group with one or two being left out, and because they have not made any special connections, they feel the exclusion more acutely. It feels like the school playground again, doesn't it? But this inclusion/exclusion has the power to take us back to those days of feeling rejected. The role of the facilitator is not to rescue, but perhaps to point out or 'mirror' what is being seen. For example:

> 'I'm becoming aware that Pete, Jenny and Mary are contacting each other outside the group and that feels like a good thing to be doing. I'm sure it offers you all some support outside. We said at the

beginning of the group that it is up to you to arrange any socializing for yourselves as we don't offer that. Friendship groups can be very comforting, but when we're in the group it would be respectful of each other not to start up your own conversations but rather for us to have a group discussion. I'm mentioning that because there were several conversations going on and I've had to break into them.'

There have been times in the life of our groups where more intimate relationships develop that have continued after the group, and some have even led to marriage. While we have been glad that people have found some relational happiness again, it has not always been easy to handle in the group, especially if the group was quite a close knit one and there were friendships forming that now have been abruptly dropped because of the other alliance. It can come as quite a shock to the facilitators when these things happen, as you are not privy to what is going on outside the group and suddenly something is possibly flaring up in the group. I have always found that an honest response is welcomed, with questioning of the group as to what might be happening in order to have a constructive discussion, if at all possible.

ABSENTEEISM AND FALLOUT

People come and go from groups for various reasons. I have tried in the initial session always to help participants understand what is expected of them. For example, it would be helpful in a closed group to know if a participant is not attending the group for a session or two. It would be helpful to have a call from them to let you know what is going on. If you have already stated that groups are not for everyone, there is a possible escape route if someone needs it. The question arises if someone does not attend and does not inform you they are not coming. You can find yourself with a dilemma: if you contact them they have to give you an explanation, and you hope that they would be brave enough to say what is going on for them. If you do not contact them, they may feel neglected. The worst scenario is if someone were to accuse us of being uncaring because no one bothered to contact to see if anything was wrong. There may be specific reasons that people have left the group and it might be constructive to know about these issues. It might have to do with the group facilitators and their style of leading; with the process that is involved; the lack of structure or too much of it; or someone else in the group. It could be that it is not the right time in their grief journey to attend the group; maybe it is just too hard to face things which being in a group has forced them to do.

It would be useful to discuss the issue of absenteeism, lateness or dropping out, and the impact it can have on the group, before the group starts. An obvious place for this to be discussed is when introducing the ground rules. Those who run open groups or drop-in groups may not feel the pressure to do this in their contracting because participants have the freedom to attend or not attend as they wish and they are not as bound by time constraints as closed groups tend to be.

I have attempted in this chapter to bring some thoughts to bear in mind when handling challenging behaviours in the group setting. When seeing someone on a one-to-one basis, these behaviours might not be as evident as they are when people join others in a group. Perhaps it is true that we really only get to know ourselves when we are in relationships. As people set out in a bereavement group they are already vulnerable and they are already using strategies they have developed, or begun to use, when they feel under pressure. It is always wise then to proceed cautiously with people and check out how they are responding and feeling, and what they are wanting from a group before they start out, as well as during the group as they progress.

It is very possible I have not addressed one of the behaviour patterns you have concerns about, as it is difficult to cover all the different behaviours that could be presented in a group. However, I hope that I have given you enough suggestions on handling a variety of behaviours that would help you feel confident enough to move towards the person who is giving you cause for concern in a gentle, caring and positive way. In the next chapter I will look at some of the pitfalls you might encounter and have not been prepared for.

CHAPTER 5

Pitfalls Along the Way

There may be some areas of difficulty in facilitating support groups that can be handled if you just have a little bit of forewarning. What they say about experience being a good teacher might be right in theory, but in practice it might be helpful to be able to think about certain situations before they happen, when you are left trying to sort out relationships, group dynamics and the practicalities of group leadership on the hoof.

PARTICIPANTS FORMING A CLIQUE AND DIVERTING THE FOCUS OF THE GROUP

Because of the more open-ended time frames in open groups than in time-limited, closed groups, cliques may be more likely to form. The scenario I will outline below demonstrates these two aspects: participants forming cliques and taking away the focus of the group from the original purposes.

When Fran took on the post of group co-ordinator at a local bereavement organization, her role was to develop the groups in the service as well as training facilitators to take on other groups. She was assured that the aim of the existing groups was to be supportive rather than social. However, one of the groups she inherited in particular seemed to have become viewed by most of the participants as a social group, with three or four of the participants, who had been attending for a long time, tending to take over the conversation and making it clear they were friends together. She had observed that these people were also inclined to start up separate conversations with one

141

another which were disruptive to the group format. Fran had tried the subtle approach once or twice and had talked endlessly about it in supervision. The tension started to rise when she tried to bring a participant back on track. Iris had spent a long time talking in great detail about how the washing machine had gone wrong, how her neighbour's cat was fouling in her garden and how her nephew's children were behaving, which seemed to be the sort of topics Iris would bring to the group. Fran explained that she thought Iris was taking time talking about these other things when she and the rest of the group might wish to address their bereavement issues. Iris complained, 'But I don't want to talk about my husband and my bereavement. I come here to get away from all those things.' At which point Fran discussed the purpose of the group again, but was faced by the two or three 'friends' who supported Iris.

There are two dilemmas here: one, the group was not fulfilling its original purpose; and the other, the safety of others who might join, would soon become an issue as the ground rules were being disregarded. The options facing Fran were not easy:

1. She could face the disapproval of the group and establish the ground rules once more, though there was already considerable resistance to her, as they regarded *her* as the newcomer into *their* group.

2. She could meet with all the participants on an individual basis and discuss the options open to them. This would be time consuming but perhaps better than having the group collectively stand against her.

3. She could ask another authority figure in the organization to attend the next group meeting, to listen to their points of view and hear them out, but to restate the policy of the organization in terms of the aims of providing support groups.

4. She could disband the group and start another group, with any from the existing group who wished to use the group for support work, and recruit more participants to attend for this purpose.

Unfortunately there was never going to be just one simple answer to this dilemma, and Fran might, of course, have no option but to work her way through these as steps in a remedial process. Very often the only recourse you have if participants are forming cliques is to confront it in the group, discuss the difficulties it presents and request that it does not happen. If it continues, then remedial action needs to be put in place.

FAMILIARITY AND OVERSTEPPING THE BOUNDARIES

There is a fine line between participants feeling comfortable in your company and in the group situation and being over-familiar with you and with others in the group. If they start to treat you as a long lost friend, maybe they have started down that route. That route can take them into a number of behaviours that can leave you feeling uncomfortable and the cohesion of the group threatened. They begin perhaps to be over-familiar in their greetings, begin making personal comments about your appearance and flattering you, singling you out to talk to you in the breaks about things they have done, and through their body language appearing to be 'pals' with you. Their behaviours could suggest to others in the group that they are more in your favour than the others are; it may give an appearance that the 'favoured' participant knows more about you than the rest do.

In places of worship it can be even more difficult to keep boundaries clear, as very often the pastoral support worker also attends services with the person who is being supported. There is undoubtedly a special place in pastoral work for encouragement and support both emotionally and spiritually. However, it can be a place for someone to become overly dependent, and even to form a strong attachment to the pastoral worker, which could possibly lead to more difficult situations arising.

These situations can arise in some instances because people who work in the area of bereavement and pastoral support do not want to offend people and do not want to appear to be too distant. It has been my experience, as I have visited many hospices around the UK, that there are cultures where it is acceptable for patients and relatives to be hugged and kissed, especially when they are feeling upset. Often patients and relatives are known over a period of time, and the intensity of the connections at poignant and sad moments seems to lend itself to these more tactile and emotional expressions.

Some congregations in places of worship also may be in the habit of kissing each other, and expressing sympathy with a hug. I understand that this is one area that is quite contentious, but I will risk causing disagreement by talking about the problem of touching and hugging.

If participants have experienced the culture where it is fine to hug and kiss on arrival and departure, there will be some who may perceive that it is acceptable to be more familiar with you and start treating you as if you are one of their extended family. However, those who are more conservative may be a little taken aback and be put off by it. Touch also means many different things to different people, and as professionals or as volunteers working in a supportive role it is probably best to err on the side of caution with regard to touch. It can be gut wrenching to sit with those whose hearts are literally breaking with grief, but a hug and a kiss is not the solution and it might lead to misunderstandings. I do believe that we can be gentle and approachable without having to touch and hug the participants. These are, after all, vulnerable people who may take the idea of touch too far in their minds, or in their behaviour. I would not say that you can, or would want to, prevent their goodbye hugs when the group has finally finished, but it is my advice that it would not be advisable to make it a regular practice during the group sessions.

In addition, time spent lingering to talk with you after the session has ended can add to the sense of over-familiarization and overstepping the boundaries. For some participants their emotional perception might be that this is the *real* contact they want. The business of the group is what happens 'in there' in a formal way, and is less satisfying for them than this informal contact. Beginnings and endings are important not only to show respect to each participant's time and commitments, but also to set the boundaries in place about what goes on in the group. Those who honour the boundaries may well feel resentful of those who stay behind and become like 'teacher's pets'. I recognize it might sound as if I am reducing people's adult responses to the playground again. However, there are those childhood memories for us all that can be evoked by simple gestures and small incidences that are reminiscent of what we experienced as children, negatively as well as positively.

On the other hand, if the participants linger to talk to each other after the group session has ended, this is no bad thing as it would indicate they are forming new friendships. But I would advise the facilitators to remove themselves so that they are not part of the socializing aspect of the group. You may have to move them on, of course, if the venue you have is to be used after the group meeting, and the group should probably be advised of this in advance. There have been group participants in my experience who have gone for lunch together after a morning session, or have met for lunch before a group starts in the afternoon. It usually takes a motivated person, a natural leader, to get this going among the group.

There are also boundaries of confidentiality that can be really difficult to handle and cause concern in a group. If the participants do start forming friendships outside the group, there may be a temptation for them to talk about what has happened in the group while they are outside. For those who have not been included in these social gatherings, there may be a feeling of insecurity arising from the concern that what they bring to the group is not safe any more. In the same way there may be concerns that confidences will be broken between those who share lifts, as sometimes happens after a group has met and they realize they live near to each other. The most normal and natural way to deal with this is to raise it in the group and to talk again of the ground rules. You could say something like:

> 'It seems that some of you are meeting up outside the group and one or two are sharing lifts, which is very kind, thank you. We're so pleased this is happening, as we would really encourage the mutual support you can find among yourselves. But I would just want to remind you about the ground rules around confidentiality. I feel sure you wouldn't want to think that anyone was talking about you behind your back outside the group, so please do remember that this holds for all of us and please keep what is said in the group inside this room.'

You may find out what is going on outside the group only when something is mentioned in the group that is new information, and you know that it must have been shared outside the group. Being alert to this means you can tackle it when it happens, so that you do not assume everyone knows, except you, and also so that everyone knows what is going on. It is important that everyone understands there is transparency about these things in the group. So the simplest way is to intervene and ask the question. For example:

'Perhaps I can just come in here? I'm wondering if I'm the only one who feels a little out of touch right now as I've just heard something that Ruth said about Sandra that I don't think I've heard from Sandra in the group. Is it possible that others don't know this and is it something that you might have shared together outside the group? It's OK if that's the case, but it would be good just to know.'

Maintaining confidentiality in a group can be really difficult, and basically we have to trust that the participants are adhering to the spirit of it and are not gossiping behind someone else's back. I have found that the more the participants appreciate and value the group, the more they seem to want to make the group experience positive for everyone, and so they are more likely to work at keeping the boundaries and ground rules.

PARTICIPANTS BEING UPSET BY A FACILITATOR'S COMMENTS

We can all be guilty of making throwaway comments or, at times, not being aware of the impact our words have on people. This can happen at any time, even given our training and experience, and is without doubt at some point likely to happen to all of us as we work with people in their vulnerable and sensitive places. I will illustrate this with the following scenario.

Sally is a very experienced group facilitator who has worked with many bereavement groups over the years. She was facilitating a group of mixed ages and a balanced mix of men and women. One of the participants was David, the oldest man in the group, who had been quite friendly and open with the other participants. However, Sally noticed that David was avoiding any depth of detail around the story of his wife's illness and death and was quite stoic in his approach to his own grief, though sensitive to others' stories and sorrows. Near the end of the third session, David revealed that he was very angry with the medical team who had attended his wife and with some of the nursing standards she had been 'subjected' to. Because of the time, and in keeping with good practice, Sally reflected what David had said, and then added, 'Because of the time constraints today, David, unfortunately we don't have much time to go too deeply into this now. And it feels too important to let it go. We'll have a look at it next time, shall we?' David looked a bit put out and responded, 'We shall, shall we?' Sally was a little taken aback by David's tone, but said, 'Well, David, it seems it's quite an issue for you, so it might be good to go over it in more depth.'

In their debrief after the session Sally talked it through with the co-ordinator of the bereavement service, and thought it might prove to be a bit of a breakthrough for David if he could bring back the anger he had expressed and process it in the safety of the group. During the week, however, the co-ordinator received a telephone call from David saying he did not think he was going to continue with the group. In the conversation that followed, the co-ordinator ascertained, after some gentle persuasion, that David had been put out with the way Sally had talked about him having an 'issue', and he did not wish to talk about the treatment of his wife in any great depth. David had felt that he had left the group under the 'threat' of having it all brought up again. The co-ordinator encouraged David to come again, as he had enjoyed the group and the other participants and realized that he would be spiting himself not to come. The co-ordinator undertook to speak to Sally and to tell her of David's discomfort. This she duly did, and Sally was able to handle it well in the session by saying at the beginning of the session, 'At the end of our session last week, David was telling us about how he felt about his wife's treatment in the hospital, but I'm not sure whether you would like to go back to that or not this week, David?' David was able to say he did not wish to, and the group moved on. As far as the others were concerned, David had been given the option as they all would have been, and they could talk or not talk, as they wished, without pressure.

This situation was rescued because David had telephoned to cancel, and was able to be honest with the co-ordinator. It does illustrate, however, how sensitive the communication can be with bereaved people when they feel put on the spot. Although Sally had done what was perfectly acceptable in suggesting that they look at David's story and issue again in more depth at the next session, it had obviously felt threatening to David, particularly so as it was in front of the others. So it is always helpful to offer people a get-out clause so that they can duck out of being in the hot seat in the group. It is also important to bear in mind that the words we use every day, even simple ones like 'issue', 'problem' and 'process' (the tools of the trade for those of us in the helping professions), may not sit well for those of an older generation or indeed for those who are not used to such language.

NOT PROVIDING A SAFE PLACE

One of the most important aspects of our group work is to ensure the group is a safe place for people to come into; a place where they can open up and share when they are able. The problem of not providing a safe place can be illustrated by the situation that faced Laura.

Laura had been facilitating an open group for some time and found that over the past year of the group's life there were people who had made particular friends and who were now tending to feel very comfortable and chatty together. There had been no newcomers to the group for a few months, and Laura was beginning to be concerned the group might not meet the needs of new participants and would not be a safe place for someone who was recently bereaved. Sadly this proved to be the case.

Before Laura could speak to them about it and explore with them the impact their behaviour might have on a newcomer, a woman in the first few months of her bereavement came for the first time. She arrived visibly anxious and late, perhaps deliberately so or perhaps due to other factors, and she sat next to Barry, who was emerging as one of the group 'leaders' and not in a positive way. Barry had begun to be more dominant of late and had started diverting the discussions away from the bereavement issues. Before Laura had a chance to introduce the newcomer and restate the ground rules, thereby starting the group in a controlled and safe way, Barry started asking the newcomer a series of questions about herself and why she was there, while the others continued to chatter over their tea. The woman, who was clearly distraught, got up and hurriedly left the room. Laura followed her out, leaving her co-facilitator with the group, but nothing Laura could say would persuade the woman to stay. Feeling terribly guilty and also angry, Laura returned to the participants, who had just gone back to meaningless chatter. Laura sat for a few minutes and then told the participants how upset she felt that the group was no longer a place where newcomers could feel welcome, safe and respected, and most importantly they seemed to have forgotten what it felt like to be vulnerable immediately after a death. She expressed her sadness and closed the group early.

Laura talked this over with her supervisor and a colleague who had worked with this particular group at times when Laura had been away and had also previously co-facilitated with her for several months. Together they decided that it would be advisable for Laura not to attend the next session but for the colleague to cover for her and address the issues. This would give the participants a chance to air their views on what had happened. In the next group session the participants shared how they felt Laura had laid the law down and some were quite cross with her. Laura's colleague listened calmly and carefully but reinforced the purpose of the group, and after that a few of the group left. Laura felt this was a very necessary pruning and was in the end for the best, as the group grew organically from that point.

Laura was confronted with some difficult group behaviours that needed addressing very quickly, and perhaps sooner rather than later in retrospect. Events overtook them and someone was left feeling bruised. Laura's experience of this group behaviour reinforced several vital factors about facilitating a group: maintaining boundaries is crucial to the well-being of the group, as is maintaining transparency about what is happening within the group dynamics, especially where participants are meeting outside the group. Maintaining focus on the group's aims and purposes is a way of helping to provide participants with a safe place in which they may choose to share.

One sign that all is not well and the group is becoming unsafe is if someone is regularly not sharing. It might be worthwhile contacting them on an individual basis and asking them if they are struggling with something in the group, or in their own life, or if there is something you can do to help them feel more secure about sharing. This would be a way of opening the discussion up. Another sign might be if one or two participants suddenly leave a group after regular attendance. It might be helpful to find out if there was something that was said or done in the group that might be corrected, or if not, something the facilitators can learn from. Unfortunately, you might learn what people really think only by sending out an evaluation questionnaire, and only then if the participants choose to return them with honest feedback.

ALLOWING A GROUP TO GO DOWN
IN THEIR MOOD EVERY WEEK

There are some groups that never seem to lift themselves off the ground week in and week out. The group participants may be people who are all too raw or too early in their grief to make the most of the group support; or they may be a mixture of people who are by nature melancholic and who do not normally have an optimistic world view – their glass has always been half empty. Whatever the case, it can be difficult to cope with this perpetual sadness. I do not wish you to misunderstand me here: the death of a loved one is a personal tragedy; life changes forever, and sadness is real and heavy for people. I would not expect a group to be full of laughter, but it seems strange to say that after a few weeks most participants are able to share a little levity about something. Perhaps they describe a particularly pleasant memory of a loved one; or an expression they used to use that has been passed down in the family; or an example of a quirky sense of humour; or something that has happened to them that causes the group to smile or laugh.

Some people though, it is true and sad to say, take on the role of the perpetual mourner; they have decided that nothing will lift their spirits ever again. If there is one, or two, like this in a group it may be possible to speak to them individually to see if they would prefer one-to-one support. As a strategy from an early point in the sessions, it may be beneficial to ask them to bring in photographs of their loved ones or anything their loved ones made or wrote or was significant to them, as this is usually a good focus. If after the fourth session in a closed group you find the mood is still very low, it would be better to talk honestly about it and to ask if there is anything the group would like to do differently, and if what is happening in the group is acceptable for everyone. It might be that they just need the fact that their mood is very dark every week to be pointed out to them and also that you are concerned they might go away feeling worse than when they came in.

SACRIFICING THE GROUP FOR
THE SAKE OF ONE PARTICIPANT

Here I need to return to my lecturer's words when I was training: 'The group is more important than the individual.' It is possible to allow the behaviour of one participant to dominate the group to such an extent that the other participants stay away and the group folds up. Early handling of the issue seems to be the answer to most difficult behaviours, with an individual meeting to discuss it wherever possible. Early on in your experience of facilitating groups this might seem like an extraordinarily difficult thing to do, but as you learn to handle the dynamics it will become clearer to you as to what needs to be done.

In the case of Barbara, who was a dominating person in the group of whom I wrote in Chapter 1, it was necessary to deal with her behaviour immediately so that the group did not disintegrate. Sometimes, however, the group just needs to fold up; maybe it has run its course and you have to let it go. The participants are also responsible for helping the group along, and so it might be necessary to let them deal with a situation in the best way they know how. Two of our team co-facilitated a closed group that ended up dwindling to two participants, partly due to the fact they were a group of extremely different people who would not have got along under normal circumstances. To be truthful, the facilitators were relieved but also disappointed when it closed, and the comments from one of the group bore out their convictions when he wrote on his feedback form that they had been a group of 'diverse and odd people'.

There are some issues that people bring into a group that might threaten the life of a group and require you to refer them on to another agency. I consider Wolfelt's (2004) list of issues, or alerting 'red flags' as he calls them, to be a reasonably good summary of what to look out for. You should be aware that not everyone will be suitable for group work and you may have to refer on at any stage in the process, either at assessment or at any other stage in the group process when you become concerned for a participant because of any of the following:

- Persistent thoughts of suicide, expressions of serious suicide intent, or the development of a specific suicide plan.

- Arriving at your group under the influence of alcohol or drugs.

- Previous diagnosis of a serious mental health disorder.

- Profound symptoms of anxiety or depression that interfere with the ability to do basic self-care.

- Uncontrollable rage directed at others.

- Physical harm to self or others.

- Uncontrollable phobias, such as an inability to be by themselves at any time.

- Characteristics of mourning (such as anger or guilt) that do not appear to change at all over a period of months.

(Wolfelt 2004, p.76)

Wolfelt's note to the above list is also worth quoting verbatim:

> *Note: the above list is not all-inclusive. You should use your good judgment as to whether or not a group member would benefit more from individual counseling than from a support group. It is also important for you as a group leader to realize that, even when you make a referral for individual counseling, the person may choose not to take your advice. (Wolfelt 2004, p.76)*

CONTROVERSIAL SUBJECT MATTER

Religious beliefs

There is an old adage that when you are in social gatherings you should avoid speaking of politics or religion. While it is rare to encounter discussions on politics in a bereavement support group, it is not uncommon to hear people talk about religion. In a group of diverse people and religions, someone may well raise the issue of their faith, their beliefs about the after-life, their visits to a medium or clairvoyant, or any other spiritual matter. For some people the issue of their faith or religion is as vital to them as breathing, and deeply impacts the way they are coping with their bereavement. Others do not wish to talk about such matters as they have no religious beliefs, nor any concept of an after-life. There may be some in fact who have had past experiences of a place of worship, a particular congregation or a leader that have left them antagonistic towards religion or any mention of spiritual things.

As an illustration, one experience Joan had with a group made her team of facilitators consider how to handle such matters before they arose in the next group. The situation was this: Joan's group had a participant, Edna, who had a strong affiliation with a religious organization and would constantly bring the subject back to her point of view and her belief system. On several occasions Joan had said, 'Edna, your beliefs seem to be very strong but they might not be shared by other participants in the group.' This had not deterred Edna though, and the group became quite uncomfortable, with people shuffling in their seats in agitation, until another participant expressed his antagonism towards such beliefs. He was careful not to make it personal to Edna, but said if these things kept on being brought up, he would think about leaving the group. It was a hard one to handle and, in the embarrassing silence that followed, Joan asked how others felt about this. They tentatively agreed with him in feeling uncomfortable with the subject being brought up as often as it had been. Edna's reaction in the group was to say, defensively, 'Well, you're all entitled to your own thoughts and beliefs, or none, as I am to mine.' Unfortunately, after the group, Edna told Joan she would not be returning, and could not be persuaded to return.

In their next team meeting, Joan and her co-facilitator raised this as an issue and the team considered putting some guidelines into their ground rules concerning the sharing of religious beliefs. They wrote this in for subsequent groups, hoping that it would be sensitively done. The wording was: 'While we acknowledge that some of you may hold strong religious beliefs, it is hoped that you will be sensitive to others who do not.' All seemed to go well until after a few groups had run and the feedback was received from several people who said they had felt stifled by the comment. They wrote that they felt they had been 'warned off', and so they felt unable to share something that was truly important to them and their bereavement. This is an aspect of leading groups that requires sensitivity and experience, and still you may not be able to satisfy everyone in the group.

You may, of course, be running a group in a place of worship where everyone is of the same faith system and it will be a matter for you and the group to negotiate as to how the group allows for people to disagree over issues of their faith. The death of a loved one can plunge people into depths of despair where they may start to question their faith and belief systems, and some may appear to lose their faith altogether. On the other hand, some may gain a faith they did not have before. I would suggest to those who run groups in places of worship that sensitivity be shown towards those who are struggling with faith. Facilitators would do well not to presume that everyone is in the same place spiritually, and it would be good to allow doubts and even anger to be expressed rather than be suppressed. The person who is deceased may have had a faith, and may have belonged to the place of worship. However, the bereaved family members who attend a group may not be believers and will have come to a group in a place of worship to receive comfort, to be understood and to be cared for. As they travel on their journey of grief, you may or may not see them come to your worship services, but they may experience the outworking of your faith through the care you offer them at the time of their greatest need. Lesley Whittaker, a counsellor and church pastoral worker who led a bereavement support group at her church for several years, explained it this way in her correspondence with me:

> *We had to be very careful with meeting on church premises and having Christians leading that we were accepting of people wherever they were with regards to faith. On the other hand, because people had received their invitation mainly through the church there was often an expectation that everything would be seen through a Christian perspective, especially with the older people who came. We did not do Bible teaching, theological discussion or prayer however, except at the memorial services that were held yearly on a Sunday evening, or at times by request with individuals, after the main part of the group had finished. (L. Whittaker, personal communication, 2011)*

She also explained that people stopped attending the group for various reasons, but mainly because they felt it had offered them what they needed, and while some people did start coming to church and getting involved in other groups, some just left and were not involved with the church after that. As there was a church pastoral team some people had home visits, with a little extra individual support, and counselling was available if there was a need. Faith issues were not pressed upon the participants and they were free to engage with those issues or not, as they wished.

Sexuality

Another aspect of life that may prove to be uncomfortable to talk about in a group would be the participants' sexuality and how they deal with this as bereaved people. I would never want to avoid this subject with a group but neither would I want to force the issue when the participants could be caused embarrassment. I have previously addressed this issue in a chapter entitled, 'There are Difficult Issues to Explore' (Graves 2009, pp.164–170). In those pages you might discover some ways of addressing the issue in a group. At one level, it might simply be enough to acknowledge the participants' loss of intimacy in their relationships. There may also be some value to thinking about running men-only groups facilitated by men, and women-only groups facilitated by women, so that this issue might be raised and discussed perhaps more openly. I am not saying that this is the answer; I simply offer it as a suggestion.

If a participant raises the issue of their sexuality, it would be as well to ask the group if this is something they also struggle with and if they would like to talk about it in this forum. If it is something they wish to discuss, it would be the facilitator's role to ensure that the participants remain feeling comfortable with how it is handled. If it is not an issue they wish to discuss, you can suggest to the participant who raised it that they meet with you outside the group to talk about it. You could also say something like:

> 'We all have our own particular struggles, and sexuality is part of everyday life and can be really missed after the death of a loved one. Very often a long illness has already impacted that part of your relationship and might have been a missing feature for some time. For others an unexpected death has suddenly robbed you of that part of your relationship. We can acknowledge here and now that this can be a struggle for some. Perhaps we can go on to think about how you find comfort when you feel lonely and sad.'

Some might consider this tactic to be avoidance of a real issue. If the group were a counselling therapy group, the topic of someone's sexuality might be an issue to be taken up and people's responses to it explored. However, in a support group, we are looking at providing support and assistance rather than causing harm or embarrassment when it is not needed.

In conclusion, through the above discussions I have made some observations about the pitfalls I wish I had been aware of before I started groups. I do believe you can only learn so much from a book and your training, and then you simply have to learn by doing it. So although this is not an exhaustive list of some of the pitfalls you might meet, they are some I have encountered along the way, for which my training and reading did not necessarily prepare me. There may be others that you have encountered or will encounter, but I hope that some of the guidance I have set out above will stand you in good stead.

Conclusion

At the outset of this book I started by saying I hoped to dispel some of the mystique around setting up and facilitating bereavement support groups. I hope that this has been accomplished and that those of you who may be new to running groups would not now think of abandoning the idea because of all that is involved.

As you have gone through the book looking for answers to the issues and concerns you might have about groups, I hope that you have found some suggestions, but you may well be putting the book down with more questions. It has been my intention to raise the issues and look at some ways forward, knowing that I do not have the definitive answers. Rather, it has been a process of pulling together my experiences and some of the issues I have come across in practice.

It might be helpful in this conclusion to highlight some of the key factors discussed in the book, so that they are emphasized and reinforced for you. In the beginning, be sure you know what it is you want to offer and that it is meeting a felt need in your community. Being aware of what you are capable of offering and what you are not able to offer will help you guide would-be participants in their choice of support. If they want a social group and you are not offering this, you should be able to tell them so and direct them to something in the area that may be more suitable. So it might be worthwhile doing a bit of research into what is in your own locality that people can take advantage of. It is important to match your facilities and resources to the people. It will also be of benefit to keep in mind the kind of group it is, either a closed group or an open group, and there are a variety of ways of operating within these that you may wish to experiment with.

Once you have sorted out your aims and know what it is you want to offer, it is important to be prepared and to be organized. If you are not a very able administrator and are not good at organization, recruit the assistance of somebody whose strength it is and whom you can trust to do the job for you. It is no shame if administration is not one of your strengths, because as a people person you may not have the kind of mind that copes well with paper. Sending out leaflets, processing the returns and keeping track of all the correspondence with people, however, needs to be done. Sorting out the bookings of rooms, times and arrangements of the venue details as well as having everything prepared before your sessions is as vital as sitting in the group and accompanying people on their journey. It is a useful habit to get into, before your groups start, to 'rehearse' the whole process in your mind, from opening the door to the participants to the end of the session. In that way you can go over all the details you will need to be aware of: doing this exercise with a pen and paper means you will be able to make a note if something comes to mind that you had not thought of – and then action it.

As I have read through the chapters, I am aware of the emphasis on having ground rules in place for participants. They can create their own rules in the first session, or you can hand them out to be read through and discussed. Whichever way you choose to operate, you will find that these are the foundations of the life of the group, offering boundaries you can return to time and time again if necessary. It may feel rather like a chore to start with and you may be aware that the participants will want to start talking and sharing their own stories. However, if you have laid the foundations at the first session, there will be safety for you and them. You will need to explain beforehand that this is what will happen in the first session so they are aware of what to expect and do not arrive ready to pour out their stories as soon as they sit down.

I am also aware that as you meet with participants in a group setting there is a call for you to be flexible in the way you operate with people, as they will take you on a journey even in one session that may fly off in different directions than the one you had in mind. This requires you to be able to negotiate your way with people; seeking their permission to go into areas that one participant may choose to go, or to defer it. You have to be flexible but at the same time firm. As we have seen, there are some behaviours that need careful handling, and you will be called upon sometimes to take action so that those behaviours do not harm the functioning of the group. It might be worth reminding yourself, though, that a group may still not become a cohesive group even though you might have done all things well.

There are various behaviours and pitfalls along the way that it would be best to be forewarned about. Not only are there difficult behaviours in the group to think about but also the alliances that can be made and the way people respond to you as a facilitator. All these can make the life of a group more challenging. My advice would be always to seek out others who are running groups and have active discussions about how to cope with difficult situations and not be afraid to share your struggles. Obviously this always has to be in the ethical framework of confidentiality.

I have the great pleasure of working with a group of highly skilled and competent volunteers who facilitate some of the groups we run at the hospice. They will say to me that they really like running groups, and some of them prefer it to individual support. Knowing, as I do, that they have all encountered difficult times and behaviours in the groups they have run, I can only believe what they tell me. So, I hope that your experience will be as profitable and satisfying. It is however a place of giving of yourself and it requires a great deal of your concentration. So I will emphasize the value and importance of good supervision, where you can discuss the issues of participants' behaviours and the issues they bring into the group in a confidential and safe place for yourself. It is important to take care of yourself, and after a group session it would be better not to try to do something that requires great things of you, like taking an exam! Even after debriefing, you can still walk away with stories and conversations that ruminate in your mind for hours after the group has gone home.

During the process of researching for and the writing of this book, I have been challenged in my own way of doing things through the conversations I have had with my colleagues who have been running their groups in different ways. Some of the challenges for me have been to think outside the box, in being more creative and flexible, and to think about ways we might, as an organization, meet the needs of more people who have been bereaved.

In the end, what we are doing is providing people with the space and the place to meet and share with others who are going through some similar struggles. We are not able to take their pain away; we are not going to solve their problems, particularly of how to live with the loss of one who was loved and is constantly missed. We are, however, able to provide a place for reflection, for recall, for remembrance and for the revisiting of memories, good as well as painful ones. This is a special offering to people who are hurting, but it will only ever be part of the picture for them; though it might be a special beginning for some of them as they meet with others and connect with each other's sorrow.

This book has been my offering to those who work with bereaved people in many settings, but I am aware that it is not a definitive text on how to work in bereavement support groups. Indeed, I am hopeful that it will be the beginning of a journey for those who have not done much group work, and that it will also be the beginning of a dialogue for all of us, as we try to support those who are hurting and who are looking to us for some answers. We know we do not have the answers, but together in a group they might be able to work out some acceptable solutions for themselves. That is our hope for them.

An Example of a Support Group's Threefold Leaflet

BEREAVEMENT SUPPORT GROUP
Information Leaflet

(Image of a group)

Bereavement Support Groups offer you the opportunity to join others who are experiencing similar losses and issues.

Contained in this leaflet are some details which you may find helpful.

Times and dates

The next eight group sessions will take place on the following dates:

We meet at:

If you are interested in attending a support group, or would like to speak to someone regarding individual support or support for children, please complete the tear-off response slip opposite and return to the Bereavement Services Co-ordinator.

RESPONSE SLIP

Return to:

What is involved in being part of a group?

- The groups usually last around eight sessions.

- It is a place to meet with other bereaved people who have experienced loss.

- There will be no set agenda or topics to discuss. It provides an opportunity to share your thoughts and feelings.

- It is *not* a social group, but often people have found that they have made new friendships during this time and wanted to socialize outside of the group. We would encourage you to do this for yourself.

Who will lead the group?

Experienced members of the Bereavement Team will lead the groups. They will be there to help you get started and to help you talk about your own personal situations.

If you wish to participate in the above bereavement support group, please complete the tear-off slip opposite and return to the address shown overleaf no later than _____

We can only run the groups if enough people let us know in time

Cont'd overleaf...

RESPONSE SLIP

Name: _____

Relative/Partner/Friend of: _____

Date of Death: _____

Address: _____

_____

Tel no: _____

I am interested in attending a Bereavement Support Group, please contact me. My preference is:

morning ☐

afternoon ☐

evening ☐

An Example of an Evaluation Questionnaire

BEREAVEMENT SUPPORT GROUP EVALUATION

Dear _____

We are writing to you now, after your group has finished, asking if you could help us evaluate the service we are offering and suggest how we could improve it. It would be helpful if you could be specific and give examples or suggestions, which we might be able to incorporate into any future group work.

Your feedback will be held in strictest confidence.

Help received in the group

1. What was the most helpful aspect of attending the group and why?

2. What was the least helpful aspect of attending the group and why?

3. Was there anything you would have expected to gain from the group that you did not gain?

Support you had from the facilitators

4. What did you feel about the facilitators and their support of you?

5.   What might you have changed about the leaders' role or support?

Practicalities

6.   How happy were you with the size of the group? Please tick.

     A.   Very happy/quite happy/unhappy. ☐

     B.   I would have preferred more/fewer in the group. ☐

7.   How did you feel about the mix of the group?

8.   Your comments about:

     (a)   The length of the group sessions.

     (b)   The frequency of the sessions.

     (c)   The duration of the group (eight weeks).

9. How practical/comfortable was the venue for you?

10. How might we improve on the group work next time?

Thank you for taking the time to complete this feedback sheet.

Name _____

Office Use Only

An Example of a Facilitator's Record

BEREAVEMENT SUPPORT GROUP FACILITATOR'S RECORD

Session no: **Date:**
Facilitator:

1. What emotional state did they appear to be in at the beginning of the session?

2. What issue did they bring into the session?

3. What has been of significance to them in this session? (Was there anything new they left with?)

4. Who do they seem to be relating to in the session and why?

5. How did they leave emotionally?

NAME	COMMENTS

References

Betley, C. (2011) Information obtained from a PowerPoint presentation given at the Cruse Bereavement Care Conference, Warwick, July 2011.

Bowden, C. (2011) 'Waves: A psycho-educational programme for adults bereaved by suicide.' *Bereavement Care 30*, 3, 25–31.

Corey, M.S. and Corey, G. (eds) (1992) *Groups: Process and Practice.* Pacific Grove, CA: Brooks/Cole.

Dies, R.R. (1983) 'Clinical Implications of Research on Leadership in Short-term Group Psychotherapy.' In M.S. Corey and G. Corey (eds) (1992) *Groups: Process and Practice.* Pacific Grove, CA: Brooks/Cole.

Graves, D. (2009) *Talking with Bereaved People: An Approach for Structured and Sensitive Communication.* London: Jessica Kingsley Publishers.

Kindred, M. and Kindred, M. (2011) *Once Upon a Group: A Guide to Running and Participating in Successful Groups.* London: Jessica Kingsley Publishers.

MacLeod, J. (1998) *An Introduction to Counselling.* Buckingham: Open University Press.

Moss, J. (2012) *Writing in Bereavement: A Creative Handbook.* London: Jessica Kingsley Publishers.

Neimeyer, R. (2011) Information obtained from a lecture given at the ABSCo Conference, Leeds, summer 2011.

Rogers, J.E. (ed.) (2007) *The Art of Grief: The Use of Expressive Arts in a Grief Support Group.* New York: Routledge.

Wolfelt, A.D. (2004) *The Understanding Your Grief Support Group Guide: Starting and Leading a Bereavement Support Group.* Fort Collins, CO: Companion Press.

Further Reading

TO RECOMMEND TO BEREAVED PEOPLE

Boydell, K. (2005) *Death…And How to Survive it: A Practical and Uplifting Guide to Coming to Terms with the Loss of Your Partner.* London: Vermilion.

Ginsburg, G.D. (1997) *Widow to Widow: Thoughtful, Practical Ideas for Rebuilding Your Life. Challenges, Changes, Decision-making and Relationships.* Tucson, AZ: Fisher Books.

Munday, J.S. (2005) *Overcoming Grief: Joining and Participating in a Bereavement Support Group.* Skokie, IL: ACTA Publications.

Noel, B. and Blair, P.A. (2008) *I Wasn't Ready to Say Goodbye: Surviving, Coping and Healing after the Sudden Death of a Loved One.* Naperville, IL: Sourcebooks.

FOR GROUP COUNSELLING

Carlson, H. (2001) *The Courage to Lead: Start Your Own Mutual Help Support Group.* Madison, CT: Bick Publishing House.

Hoy, W.G. (2007) *Guiding People Through Grief: How to Start and Lead Bereavement Support Groups.* Crawford, TX: Grief Connect.

Hughes, M. (1995) *Bereavement and Support: Healing in a Group Environment.* Washington, DC: Taylor & Francis.

Kurtz, L.F. (1997) *Self-help and Support Groups: A Handbook for Practitioners.* Thousand Oaks, CA: Sage.

MacLeod, D. (2007) *Seasons of Hope: Creating and Sustaining Catholic Bereavement Groups.* Notre Dame, IN: Ave Maria Press.

Tudor, K. (1999) *Group Counselling.* London: Sage.

FOR CHILDREN'S GROUP WORK

Lehmann, L., Jimerson, S.P. and Gaasch, A. (2000) *Grief Support Curriculum: Facilitator's Handbook*. Philadelphia, PA: Brunner-Routledge.

GENERAL READING

Neimeyer, R.A., Darcy, L.H., Winokeur, G.R. and Thornton, G.F. (2011) *Grief and Bereavement in Contemporary Society*. New York: Routledge.

Useful Resources

(All information was correct and all websites functioning in March 2012.)

CENTRE FOR THE GRIEF JOURNEY
www.griefjourney.com

A website providing information about the programmes run by Dr Bill Webster. It offers DVDs and books that could be of use in a closed group with structured content.

COMPASSIONATE FRIENDS
www.tcf.org.uk

53 North Street
Bristol BS3 1EN

National UK Helpline: 0845 123 2304

Supporting bereaved parents and their families. A self-help group for parents who are bereaved of children of any age.

CRUSE BEREAVEMENT CARE
www.crusebereavementcare.org.uk
Youth Involvement Project: www.rd4u.org.uk

PO Box 800
Richmond, Surrey TW9 1RG

Daytime UK Helpline: 0844 477 9400
Email: helpline@cruse.org.uk

To locate local branches and obtain information about groups and training.

MERRYWIDOW
www.merrywidow.me.uk

This website provides a guide for those newly bereaved, a message board, and other useful information.

MUCHLOVED

www.muchloved.com

A memorial website that also offers a community forum for different types of losses, such as the loss of a partner or a child. It also offers support and information.

NING

http://uk.ning.com

A facility for creating your own social website which offers different pricing plans.

SOBELL HOUSE STUDY CENTRE

www.sobell-house.org.uk

Churchill Hospital
Oxford OX3 7LJ

Tel: +44 (0) 1865 225886
Fax: +44 (0) 1865 225599

The study centre offers a day's course for this purpose: 'Setting up and facilitating bereavement support groups'. Contact the centre for details of when courses run.

WAY FOUNDATION

www.wayfoundation.org.uk

A website for bereaved young men and women under the age of 50, which provides self-help information and a social and support network for adults and children.

WAY UP

www.way-up.co.uk

This is a self-help group for people bereaved of a partner and who are over 50.

Index